Endorsemen

Dr Nkiru's book is one that makes a dream come true—a sincere, truthful book that proves that our creator wants us whole mentally, emotionally, physically, and spiritually because, for a moment in time, God forsook His only begotten Son that we may be made whole.

It is the love that God has for us that delivered Dr Nkiru from mental and emotional distress that plagued her for years in the form of clinical depression. This is an experience that everyone suffering from mental, emotional, physical, or spiritual distress should desire. Dr Nkiru, a medical practitioner, proves that God's life-changing love is effective in bringing wholeness.

We know that scriptures, which are spirit and life with the ability to bring themselves to pass, are not the product of scientific investigation or human reasoning, but we can scientifically apply scriptures to bring about healing emotionally, behaviourally, and mentally.

Dr Nkiru, like many others, including myself, is living proof. Read and study this book, meditate, and experience wholeness.

Dr Christina Browne, consultant psychiatrist

The book *Overcoming Depression, Living with Joy* is a must-read for anyone who has ever felt depressed or down in spirit and wants to overcome depression and have a heart that is filled with joy at all times.

The words of this book are real and captivating. They ministered to my spirit, letting me know that as a child of my heavenly Father, He is for me, in me, and on my side to help me overcome all of life's hurdles.

This book is inspired by the Holy Spirit and is not only for those who fight depression but also for those who want to successfully win those battles in their minds and make being victorious a lifestyle. As we know, the Devil goes about like a roaring lion seeking whom he may devour, and this starts from the mind. But praise God, he's already a defeated foe.

Overcoming Depression, Living with Joy goes in-depth and teaches the reader about the human make-up and how we are created in the image and likeness of God. The reality of this makes one stand tall, victorious, and complete in God, without any condemnation.

With this book, you will learn how to overcome negative thoughts and silence the Devil when he tries to sneak in. You will begin to see yourself in the image of God, as God's own offspring, created in His image and likeness, and then you will begin to live like it.

Faith Ihongbe

OVERCOMING DEPRESSION, LIVING WITH JOY

(A BIBLICAL VIEW)

DR. NKIRU OLUWATOSIN

WESTBOW
PRESS®
A DIVISION OF THOMAS NELSON
& ZONDERVAN

Copyright © 2021 Dr. Nkiru Oluwatosin.

All rights reserved. No part of this book may be used or reproduced by any means, graphic, electronic, or mechanical, including photocopying, recording, taping or by any information storage retrieval system without the written permission of the author except in the case of brief quotations embodied in critical articles and reviews.

WestBow Press books may be ordered through booksellers or by contacting:

WestBow Press
A Division of Thomas Nelson & Zondervan
1663 Liberty Drive
Bloomington, IN 47403
www.westbowpress.com
844-714-3454

Because of the dynamic nature of the Internet, any web addresses or links contained in this book may have changed since publication and may no longer be valid. The views expressed in this work are solely those of the author and do not necessarily reflect the views of the publisher, and the publisher hereby disclaims any responsibility for them.

Any people depicted in stock imagery provided by Getty Images are models, and such images are being used for illustrative purposes only.
Certain stock imagery © Getty Images.

Scripture taken from the King James Version of the Bible.

Scripture taken from the Amplified Bible, Copyright © 1954, 1958, 1962, 1964, 1965, 1987 by The Lockman Foundation. Used with permission.

Scripture quotations taken from the Amplified® Bible (AMPC),
Copyright © 1954, 1958, 1962, 1964, 1965, 1987 by The Lockman Foundation
Used by permission. www.Lockman.org

Scripture taken from the New King James Version® Copyright © 1982 by Thomas Nelson. Used by permission. All rights reserved.

Scripture taken from The Message. Copyright © 1993, 1994, 1995, 1996, 2000, 2001, 2002. Used by permission of NavPress Publishing Group.

ISBN: 978-1-6642-3629-5 (sc)
ISBN: 978-1-6642-3631-8 (hc)
ISBN: 978-1-6642-3630-1 (e)

Library of Congress Control Number: 2021911266

Print information available on the last page.

WestBow Press rev. date: 06/02/2021

This book is dedicated to the following:

My Father God; without whom I am nothing. What a joy it is to be called your daughter. Thank you, Father, for being my shield, my glory, and the lifter of my head. Thank you for making my life beautiful.

To my awesome husband, Mayowa—my friend for all times, my confidant, and my codreamer. Thank you for all your support, and thank you for always fanning my flames. Life has been even more beautiful with you. You are God-sent.

To my son, Fijinoluwa, you are such a blessing to me. The spark you light in my heart with your smile is worth every day of having you. I love you, my son. I have loved you since the first day we knew about you.

To my unborn children, I love you all already so much, and I speak into your lives always.

To my dear family, my late father, my mum, and my siblings, thank you for never giving up on me, for being there for me, and for standing firm in your faith through the trying times. I would not have made it without you all. I love you all dearly.

CONTENTS

Acknowledgements ix
Foreword xi
Preface xv

Chapter 1   My Story 1
Chapter 2   Writing Your Own Story 15
Chapter 3   What Depression Really Is 20
Chapter 4   Freedom from a Poor Self-Image 28
Chapter 5   Freedom from Fear, Anxiety, and Worry 33
Chapter 6   Freedom from Failure 40
Chapter 7   Freedom from Disappointment 44
Chapter 8   Freedom from Guilt 48
Chapter 9   Freedom from Regret 52
Chapter 10 Freedom from Indecision and Confusion 57
Chapter 11 Freedom from Hurts 62
Chapter 12 Freedom from Grief 68
Chapter 13 Living With Joy: Abiding In Love 74
Chapter 14 Living With Joy: Knowing Your Identity 80
Chapter 15 Living with Joy: The Power of Praise and
                Thanksgiving 84
Chapter 16 Living with Joy: The Power of Thoughts 89
Chapter 17 Living with Joy: The Power of Words 93
Chapter 18 Living with Joy: The Power of Vision 100
Chapter 19 Living with Joy: Light Up Your World 105
Chapter 20 Living with Joy: Enjoying Your Days 108
Chapter 21 Overcoming Depression and Living with
                Joy: A Medical Perspective 113
Chapter 22 Living with Joy: Knowing You Are Not Alone 127

ACKNOWLEDGEMENTS

"I would like to say thank you to a dear brother and friend Ifoghale Efeturi who helped me put my initial thoughts together and gave structure and form to my first written manuscript making it a lot easier to submit to my publishers".

FOREWORD

Dr Nkiru is a woman full of faith who has a heart to see people walk in the fullness of life in Christ. Her love for God is infectious. She is bold, confident, and obviously intelligent. So the question I find most people asking after hearing these descriptions is "How could someone like this have gone through depression?"

This is what sets this book apart from other books. The tripartite nature of humankind is explicitly dealt with.

Many believers struggle between medical prognosis and the application of faith, but Dr Nkiru has shown practical ways to deal with these issues. She shares her experiences, not discounting medical intervention but rather putting forward the aspects that most people miss out on.

Most people focus on the medical condition only, while others focus only on the spiritual aspect. Seeing that we are made up of spirit, soul, and body, it is impossible to find a lasting and effective solution without engaging with these three parts of a person. This is what Dr Nkiru has done so beautifully. She starts by dispelling any preconceived notions we might have of people who suffer from depression. She takes us through the depths—the ins and outs of depression—sharing her own story and capturing her own triggers and the situation that landed her in hospital.

This book is full of practical scientific and biblical principles that will liberate the reader. Everyone goes through different types of mental health challenges. It is a spectrum that many people travel through in life.

There is something for everyone to learn in this book. I particularly love the chapter that covers an incident with the author's husband and the conflict resolution skill that was displayed. Another story I love is the one about Fiji's haircut. Here we are made to see how easily one can move from having a thought to finding oneself stuck in a rabbit hole. A trail of thoughts can pull one down, leaving one wondering how one got there in the first instance.

To God's glory, this book is packed with the truth that sets people free. As you read through the revelations the author received through this amazing journey, you will be walking out of any situations that have held you bound, instead walking into your freedom and joy everlasting.

For those who are not going through any mental health issues, you will be energized and strengthened in your faith as Dr Nkiru reminds us of our identity in Christ and the revelation of God's love for us. This is a power-packed book that deserves to be in every household.

Thank you, Nkiru, for writing this book. I see 2 Corinthians 1:3–4 at work in your life:

> Blessed be the God and Father of our Lord Jesus Christ, the Father of sympathy (pity and mercy) and the God [Who is the Source] of every comfort (consolation and encouragement), Who comforts (consoles and encourages) us in every trouble (calamity and affliction), so that we may also be able

to comfort (console and encourage) those who are in any kind of trouble or distress, with the comfort (consolation and encouragement) with which we ourselves are comforted (consoled and encouraged) by God.

I believe God never wastes our pain. He walks us through the rivers and fires of affliction to bring us out with shouts of joy. We are made to walk in the shoes of those whom we are also called to serve. This process always births compassion in us and helps us introduce our Father as a mighty deliverer. Well done, Nkiru.

Shalom,
Adeola Bode-Odeyemi
Author & Prophetic Voice
www.morglobal.org

PREFACE

My name is Nkiru Oluwatosin. I am a God lover, a wife, a mum, and a doctor.

I wrote this book because I want to see people all over the world free from depression, living their lives with joy daily.

This book has come from a place of winning the battle against depression in my life with God's help and wanting to see so many more people win.

I have written this book with the Christian struggling with depression in mind, but I know this book will help anyone who doesn't know Jesus yet but is willing to come to Him and be taught by Him.

As I share what I have learnt from my personal journey and those of many people I have encountered, I pray that you will find hope and be encouraged not to give up, but to be expectant for all that God still has ahead for you.

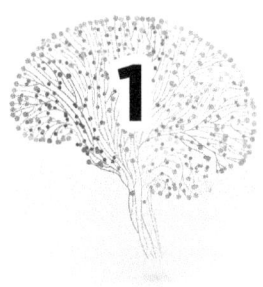

MY STORY

I would like to begin by sharing my story with you, after which I will go on to speak to you about what God has placed in my heart for you. I wrote this story for the first time on 23 October 2018. In a span of one week, I heard three times that I needed to write my story. The first time, I heard it in my spirit, and it was confirmed twice after that. The second time I heard God speak to me was while I was listening to a message, and the third came when I went to a friend's church. On all three occasions, there was an emphasis on "tell your story." I immediately knew it was time to start sharing my story to help other people come out of the pits of depression.

I needed to document what I had experienced. It was important I did so, because lives needed to be saved. I kept hearing that "there are people who think they can no longer continue with their lives. They think they are so far gone. They need to know that there is hope. There are also people who are on that journey headed downwards, towards the darkness of depression, who need to be stopped in their tracks."

I write this knowing how much I, too, longed to hear or read about anyone who had gone through something similar to what I had been through and who had come out of it successfully. I needed to know it was possible. I also write this to document God's goodness and grace. David says in Psalm 9:1b (NKJV), "I will praise you, O Lord, with my whole heart; I will tell of all your marvellous works." In Mark 5:19 (KJV), Jesus says to a man He just restored, "Go home to thy friends, and tell them how great things the Lord hath done for thee, and hath had compassion on thee."

Below is a summary of my experience from 2008 to 2009. It is my story of how God delivered me from the depths of depression.

Growing Up

As a child, I had a tendency to walk in self-pity. I remember crying as a child and telling myself nobody loved me. I would lock myself away and cry, feeling sorry for myself. All these feelings were lies the enemy had been planting. I remember my mother telling me on many occasions, "Nky, God loves you and so do we." For a little while I would believe this, but as I grew up to become a teenager and a young adult, I had not really learnt God's love for me. I suffered from low self-esteem. I tried to fight this off, but I later realized that in trying to do this in my strength, I would walk in pride because I tried to glorify myself in the struggle for acceptance.

I was also a very worried person. I did not realize how anxious and fretful I had become as the years went by. I always liked to have things under my control. I was always trying to figure things out. If I did not have it all figured out, I would not be peaceful. I took offence so easily. Throughout this time, however, God had always been there. I had always had a heart for Him. I loved the Bible stories and enjoyed reading them as a child. At some point in my second year of junior secondary school (the equivalent of year eight in the United Kingdom), I received Jesus personally. God was important to me, and I loved Him.

You may be asking yourself why I had these negative tendencies. You may be wondering whether I had a specific negative experience growing up as a child or had something particularly terrible happen to me. Well, I cannot tell you that anything specific happened to me that caused me to think the way I thought. This was inherent. You see, every single one of us has something that is at work in us that causes us harm, and this is called a sin-based nature; this is why everyone needs Jesus.

When we receive Jesus, we instantly become born again in our spirits, but our minds have to be renewed. My wrong thinking patterns still existed. This had an effect on me in my third year of secondary school. I had moments of depression born out of these wrong thinking patterns, but these periods lifted. I was always able to come out of them. Father God brought the right people around me, and somehow I never did sink that low.

My life was OK. I had and do have a wonderful family. My family was a Bible-believing and praying one. I was in no way deprived. I attended an elite primary school, Corona Nursery and Primary School in Lagos, Nigeria. I had good friends, and I was doing well in secondary school. In my final year of secondary school, I was made head girl. I did really well in my SSCEs, making 6A1s and some Bs. I got admitted into a private medical school in Nigeria, Igbinedion University, to study medicine. I made new friends, and I enjoyed my fellowship, Christian Fellowship International (CFI), which was where I gathered with other believers while in school. In my life, there really wasn't anything going on that should have made me to be so negative and have such a poor view of myself, but you see, my lack of being thankful darkened my mind and gave me a negative mindset towards God, myself, and life.

Even though I loved God, there was still some work I needed to do in renewing my mind and truly receiving God's love for me. These issues were not completely dealt with, so the enemy still had an entry point he could use. You can call this the sin that so easily besets. Even at that time, I would still have moments when I just felt so sorry for myself. I would think of everything I felt was wrong in my life and, in so doing, make myself feel so sad. During these moments, I was not being thankful. I was not giving glory to God for every good thing. I did not realize this at the time; I just felt I was being realistic.

One way I got out of these periods was with music. I loved to listen to gospel music, and I loved to dance. Most people within the Christian community in school then knew "Nkiru the Dancer." I danced to worship God. I loved to dance to praise Him. It honoured Him and lifted me. It was a case of the garment of praise for the spirit of heaviness (Isaiah 61:3). In dance, I could see myself right in front of the Father, dancing. On many occasions, I was approached by people who felt the tangible presence of God during these moments of dance. I am saying all these things because inasmuch as I still struggled with my wrong thinking habits, I loved God and loved His presence; but as I said, I had not let my mind become renewed with God's Word in the areas of worry, moodiness, and anxiousness.

The Downturn

I had been negative for so long, and recent happenings in my life worsened this. To be more specific, I came to a point in my life when I had to make a major decision about a relationship I was in, and my mental state was already so poor. I kept going back and forth on what to do. I could not bring myself to make a decision. This was caused by and fuelled by the fact that depression had already set in and was affecting my mind. The indecision and confusion with the underlying anxiety and worry finally pushed me to a breaking point. I did not realize this had become despair until the moment I realized I couldn't be happy even if I wanted to. Suddenly I realized nothing could make me happy. I tried to be happy, but I could not feel joy inside, and this kept going on and on. One day I woke up and my thoughts were racing. I felt as if I had lost control over my thinking. My heart had become so full of despair and gloom. I had slipped into severe depression.

It was so difficult to do even mundane things, as I had lost all motivation. The weight of depression felt so heavy. I could not face my day with expectations or hope. I struggled to get through each day. I had no taste for food and lost so much weight. It was fearful. I had to leave school at the time. I was in medical school, and we had major examinations coming up, but I had to leave for home. I was not coping. At home, my family could not understand what was happening. I was a shadow of myself. I can't quite put in words how dark depression can be. If you are going through this right now, please do not despair. I know how you feel. Do not give up. I can assure you that there is hope for you.

At a certain time, I felt as though I would never get my joy back. The future looked bleak. It felt as if I were in a pit with something heavy sitting on me, with thick fear and hopelessness surrounding me. I can understand why people who go through things like this may take their lives—because they are filled with an alarming and huge sense of hopelessness, sadness, fear, and inexplicable guilt. These feelings are real for the individual who is depressed to such an extent that a miracle or medications are needed to get through this, and most times medications are just not enough.

My life as I knew it was slipping away from me. I didn't think I could make it. It was so overwhelming. I lost track of time. Day and night did not make sense to me any more. I knew God as much as I thought I did, but now I needed to know Him as my healer. I knew I had no chance outside Him. My hopelessness brought me to a point where I felt that either God was who He says He is or my life was over. I felt the way David did in Psalm 38:6: "I am troubled; I am bowed down greatly; I go mourning all the day long."

Path to Healing and Victory

Being a born-again child of God, amidst the dark cloud and all that I was facing, I was still able to pray. The Holy Spirit had always been speaking. He had never wanted me to come to this point. He had tried to get me to renew my mind a long time before this, through messages I heard and many books I had read, such as Joyce Meyer's *Battlefield of the Mind*. Ah! Now I was at a loss, and I longed to run into the arms of my heavenly Father. I longed to hear His voice so I could just listen and get out of the darkness! God never left me. He never left! The moment I started seeking His voice to listen to and respond to, I heard Him.

The first thing God established in my heart was that He loved me! Hallelujah! The Spirit of God brings the word of God to our remembrance (John 14:26). I remembered Romans 8:35–39, which says *nothing* will be able to separate me from the love of my Father. I still remember that moment; in the midst of such an overwhelming presence of fear, I was seeing things move. I was hallucinating, and I remember calling a dear friend of mine. While he encouraged me, the Spirit of God brought that word of love to my mind in Romans 8: "Nothing can separate me from His love."

"God loves me! God loves me!" I screamed. "He loves me! He loves me!"

I knew my life would not and could not be over. He loved me too much to let me go. "For I am persuaded, that neither death, nor life, nor angels, nor principalities, nor powers, nor things present, nor things to come, nor height, nor depth, nor any other creature, shall be able to separate us from the Love of God, which is in Christ Jesus our Lord" (Romans 8:38–39).

Ah! I remember being so full of hope in that moment. I suddenly knew, as never before, that I was loved by the Father and that it was not over for me. He loves me too much to let me fade away. He loves me! Oh, He loves me! I can never be too far out of the reach of His love! The darkness cannot swallow me!

I got reminded of scriptures like Psalm 139:8, in which David says, "If I make my bed in hell, behold, thou art there." Wow! God loved me so much. He won't leave me even if I wilfully walk into the depths of depression. Even if I hadn't listened, and even if it looked impossible at the moment, I would still be fine. The love of God began to be revealed to me. I knew that God loved me so much that this could not be my end. Then the Holy Spirit continued to show me more scriptures! The scriptures literally came alive for me. They were all I had. They were my oxygen for my next breath.

Days went on to weeks, and weeks went on to months. I knew God loved me, and I knew I was coming out and the Holy Spirit was just working with me. I was so yielded! I was praying in the Spirit, speaking in tongues most of the time I prayed, because my mind was just a clutter and I could not believe every thought that came through it. I believed only the word of God in my heart. That was the only reality I knew was true. "For he that speaketh in an unknown tongue speaketh not unto men, but unto God … He that speaketh in an unknown tongue edifieth himself" (1 Corinthians 14:2, 4).

The power of speaking in other tongues, for the believer, cannot be underestimated. I continued to pray in the Spirit, and I began to hear God so much better. It was during this time, when I prayed in tongues the most time in my life up to that time, that the presence of

God became so strong and real to me, and I was able to walk in the gift of the word of knowledge for the first time. I would know things about people without them telling me, and this was information for their comfort. Now God has told me things about people that I had absolutely no way of knowing on my own. He told me these things so I could use them to bless people. This supernatural information comes when I spend time praying in the Spirit.

You see, as I mentioned earlier, the human being is spirit, soul, and body. The soul is the place of the mind, will, and emotions. This part of me was in chaos, but praise God, my spirit man was alive in Christ. Amidst the chaos, when my mind was playing tricks on me and I could not decipher what was or what wasn't, owing to the confusion going on in my mind, the word of God was my light. It was my path, and it was the authority I submitted my mind to. I did only what the Word said to do. This is why I remained safe and the enemy could not completely take over. I'll give you an example.

There are moments when a person who is severely depressed can get very angry during a psychotic phase. On one occasion, I was angry and I began to walk away from home. I did not know where I was going, but I stormed off angrily. People can go off like this and turn up somewhere and not realize how they got there. In psychiatry this is called a fugue. This time, just while I was storming off, my dad called out to me to come back, and I heard in my spirit, "Honour your father and mother. It's your dad talking." I immediately calmed down and listened to him.

On another occasion, it seemed as if I could not pick out my thoughts. It felt as though there were other thoughts in my mind that were not mine. I then remembered the Word of God, which says, "My sheep know my voice and the voice of another they would not follow." I immediately knew what to listen to by the leading of God, and I ignored everything else.

On more than one occasion, I saw things move. The medical world would call this hallucination. My mind was playing tricks on me. The Devil tried so hard, but I remembered the scripture that says, "Though I walk through the valley of the shadow of death, I will fear no evil." I remembered the word that says, "The fruit of the spirit is self-control", amongst other things, and also the word that says, "The spirit of a prophet is subject to the prophet." When I remembered this, I absolutely refused to give in to the strong forces trying to get me to lose control. I did not know how long this fight would last, but I knew deep down within me that I would come out on top because God said so!

The Spirit of God continued to show me what to do. He showed me Jonah 2:8: "They that observe lying vanities forsake their own mercy." I realized that Jesus had shown me mercy in that He died for my sins and bore my sicknesses and diseases. If I were going to receive healing in my mind, I would need to believe this and stand against the enemy until I saw my healing materialize. Otherwise, I would be forsaking His great mercy towards me. I had to ignore the symptoms I felt. I absolutely stopped considering them. I had raging headaches that made me feel as though my head would explode; my thoughts ran wild, and I felt as if I could not stay peaceful, but I blatantly ignored all this and continued to say under my breath, "God has not given me the spirit of fear but the spirit of power of love and of a sound mind. I have a sound mind. I have a sound mind." I said this so many times during that period that I could never count how many times I said it even if I tried.

If I had given in to the symptoms I felt, and if I had acknowledged them, I do not think I would have made it out. The depths of severe depression can be very low, and I experienced this. I fought the symptoms of delusions, hallucinations, mutism, and derealization. As I mentioned earlier, as a born-again Christian, one's spirit man is made new in Christ. As such, regardless of what had happened with my emotions and intellect, my spirit was kept from all the confusion and turmoil, and I reached into the power resident in me by Jesus. This is why it is tough for an unbeliever to come through this, and this is why many people kill themselves. I have heard about believers who have hurt themselves because they felt they couldn't go on. I know the struggle, but if only they had just held on …! This is a fight, and although they will be with the Lord, if you don't fight and you give up, the enemy will take hold.

I had been offered medications to carry on long-term with, but I refused to go on with them. Please, I mean no discredit to anyone who uses medications. I understand the depths of this problem, and I knew I had sunk so low that in the long term, the type of medications I was being offered would keep me stuck in a way I did not want for myself, and I would never be free the way I wanted to be while I was taking them. I wanted to be able to live without medications. I wanted my freedom to be complete. As a doctor, I know medications help, but if the negative thought patterns are not addressed, many people find that the medications no longer work; this is because the core issues have not been dealt with.

I just recently asked an America-based psychiatrist friend of mine what the prognosis is for a patient who is severely depressed with complications like those I have mentioned I had, and she said medications are usually required for life. Praise God! It has been thirteen years, and I have not needed any medications for depression. I just made a choice at some point that if God says I am the healed, and if His Word says I was healed by the stripes of Jesus, then I am healed and I don't care how I feel, because it is impossible for God to lie. The scripture says that by two immutable things (God's word and His promise), it is impossible for God to lie (Hebrews 6:17–18). So at His word, I am healed, and that is all I need. Once I made this resolution in my heart, I took my healing, and everything I did and said was as though I was completely free. I did not wait to feel it. I knew something had shifted in the Spirit.

I spoke to myself. I told myself to be happy. I told my mind to be calm and well balanced like the scripture says in 2 Timothy 1:7 (AMP). I was still fighting, and I did not know when I would see the manifestation, but I told God that I did not care how long it took; I was going to fight and stand on His promise until I saw it. I felt like an actor. I would laugh when I did not feel any emotion. Life still appeared bleak. I would try to study even when my mind felt so heavy and foggy and I still found it difficult to concentrate. I still had lots of medical exams ahead, and I did not know how I would make it through, except for the fact that "God said."

At the time, I remember going for a Loveworld Ministry (Loveworld is a Christ Embassy ministry in Nigeria) event with a friend. I was fully focused on listening to the Word and surrounding myself with the Word in those days. At some point in the event, the minister, Pastor Chris Oyakhilome, said, "the darkness will bow," and I suddenly knew he was talking to me. I said to myself, "Lord, is that me?" And Pastor Chris repeated it again as if he heard me ask, and he said, "Yes, you. The darkness will bow." Ah! That encouraged me so much. During those times, God gave me specific words. He told me He would give me double for the trouble I was going through. He told me that just as it had happened to Shadrach, Meshach, and Abednego when they entered the fire, they came out with not even the smell of smoke. He said no one would ever know what I had been through because there would be absolutely no sign or scar left on me.

I remember hearing Bishop David Oyedepo, a preacher in Nigeria, say, "Your life is over only when you decide it is over; for with God all things are possible." I remember needing to hear the Word constantly. I recall requesting of a friend who walked past me after fellowship in school to let me use her iPod briefly to listen to any message she had, and she gave it to me. The first message I played happened to be by Bishop Oyedepo, and it turned out to be a message regarding declaring words of breakthrough against depression! Wow, wow, wow! So timely. I listened to Joel Osteen talk about how bright my future was and how all I had to do was not give up, and believe God. The Word of God was on replay always. Cece Winans's album *Throne Room* was my heart's cry to the Father. It had been really dark, and my family had watched in despair. In fact, before this time, I had not seen my dad cry before, but during this time I saw him cry. My mum and my siblings cried also because Nkiru had become a shadow of herself. But by the grace of God, soon enough, light shined. Light shined and continued to shine, and it got brighter and brighter!

The Pivotal Role of a loving Family

Very key to my story of healing and victory is the role my family played in supporting me with their consistent love, through speaking truth to me and through their prayers. I cannot overemphasize how important it is to have a strong network of people in your life to love and be loved by. When I was in hospital, I had family present every day.

I remember waking up from being sedated and seeing my younger sister Akwugo sitting by my side. She had been seated there for hours on end. I remember my elder sister Chinelo stirring me up to pray at the start, when I didn't realize the gravity of the battle I was facing. She urged me to fight! She urged me early on to speak in tongues! My dad wanted the best for me. He did all he could to help me get better. His friend was the psychiatrist in charge of my care. Dad and the rest of the family wanted me well, and they did everything they knew to do to provide the support I needed. My mum prayed for me and with me. She agreed with me on every move I made. She was a rock of support all the way. She stood in faith with me when I told her I wanted to leave the hospital and I wanted to stop the drugs. Chinweoke, my eldest sister; my elder brother Nnamdi; and my immediate elder sister, Uzo, were all very instrumental throughout this period, speaking with me, praying with me, and encouraging me.

There were lots of tears and prayers and support. God worked with family to help me. At every point in life, please hold your networks close. Relationships are to be treasured; they are God's gift to you.

If you are not the one depressed but you are reading to know better how to help someone who is, please don't give up on your loved one. Stay close to your loved one. Keep praying for your loved one, but love him or her enough to speak the truth in love. Sometimes your loved one may need to be jolted into the realization that he or she needs to wake up to the fight for his or her mind. Don't allow your loved one to wallow in defeat. Give hope, speak life.

The presence of community in the life of a person struggling with depression is lifesaving.

I cannot say exactly how it happened; all I know is that as I pushed on and stood on the Word, change began to happen. My mind became clearer, my emotions returned, and my thoughts became calm and settled. Peace and joy were returning to me. I was able to take my exams, and I passed them. Not only that, but I succeeded in completing a medical elective in New York for eight weeks, and then I came back, continued with my studies, got to my final year, passed, and graduated from medical school! My goodness! As each day went by, it was just as though nothing had happened to me. A doctor who had seen me earlier during that period saw me when I graduated and was doing a postgraduate exam in a university in Lagos, Nigeria. I saw a look of compassion on her face when I excitedly approached her. She thought I had started medical school all over again, and I said to her, "Oh, no! I am done with that." She could not believe it because she knew how bad things for me were then. Isn't God good? Thank you, Father!

I have since gone on to practise medicine in the United Kingdom, and I am currently a primary care physician. I am married to an absolutely amazing man who was my classmate in medical school, and I have a wonderful son. My life is beautiful, and God was true to His word. I have been free from depression for thirteen years and have never looked back. Today I look around me at my family; my siblings who were there for me; and my loving mother and my late dad, who never gave up on his belief that I would make it; and my heart is full. I'm so glad they did not give up and I did not give up.

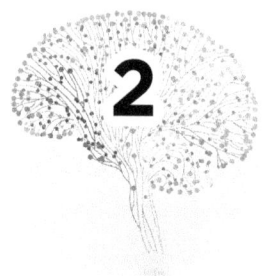

2

WRITING YOUR OWN STORY

I understand that your story is not mine, but you can write your own story of victory beginning today. I know that what you have experienced may be different from my experience, but you may similarly be finding yourself feeling hopeless, as I felt then. You may be in a position in which you think about tomorrow and it is a blur. Your mind may be filled with a fog. There may be a heaviness weighing you down so much you can barely concentrate. Even worse, you may think there is no point to living. You might be at the brink of going into despair from depression. If this is your experience, I want you to know that you are never beyond the love of God.

David said in Psalm 139:8, "If I make my bed in hell, behold, thou art there." You cannot outdo or outrun God's love. All you need to do is make a decision to choose life and live. Nothing else can stop you once you have made that decision to overcome and live with joy.

Establishing the Rights to Your Freedom

I understand that some people who may pick up this book may not be Christians, but I believe that if God has made it such that you are holding this book, then you will be blessed by the precious words in it.

Firstly, I must get you to a point where you have the rights to lay hold of the truth of the love of God and declare boldly the desire of Father God over your life. The only way you can go on affirming the Father's love is if you are His child. This is the most important decision you will make in all your life.

God is love, but God is holy. We all sinned and fell short of His glory. The wages, or the requirements, for sin is death. This death means separation from God. It means a cutting off from the life of God, with no access to Him. Praise God; He loved us so much with such a great love that He sent His Son, Jesus, who suffered for us; took our sin, shame, pain, guilt, sickness, and failures; and died for us on the cross, taking the punishment that we deserved. Jesus then rose again, and now He sits at the right hand of the Father, glorified and making intercession for us, causing us to be justified and accepted before the Father, giving us right standing with God, and breaking every barrier and hindrance to our relationship with God.

Now, we can call God our Father and boldly come to Him without any condemnation, being assured that we are perfected forever as sons and daughters of the living God! Hallelujah! All anyone has to do is believe in the name of Jesus and say verbally that He died for him or her and rose again, making the person right in God's eyes. Whoever does this immediately becomes a receiver of the grace of God and of the free gift of righteousness or right standing with God. He or she becomes a child of God. Now, God the Father did not just leave us here. When Jesus left, God sent His Holy Spirit to dwell in us and be with us forever and empower us to live the new life He has given us by our faith in Jesus.

If you haven't made the decision to believe, now is the time to believe the Father's love, to believe in Jesus and what He did on the cross, and to ask the Holy Spirit to come in and fill you.

Becoming a Child of God

If you have not accepted Jesus as your Lord and Saviour, now would be the best time to simply say, "Lord Jesus, I believe you came to earth and died for me and you rose again to make me right with God. Right now, I accept you as my Lord and Saviour. Come into my heart. Father God, thank you for making me your [son/daughter]."

If you just said that prayer, praise God! Welcome to the family of God! There is joy in heaven right now over you! Now you can be assured that you can take everything I tell you and expect results in your life!

If you are reading this and you are going through an unexplainable weight of depression or any other situation that seems insurmountable and you think it is over for you, *do not give up!* Or, if you are the anxious, worried, fretful person who is often negative and does not love himself or herself, I urge you to first believe in the love of God for you in Christ Jesus. Jesus took your sin, shame, pain, grief, and sickness. His love for you is as high as the heavens are above the earth, and He has taken your sin away from you as far as the East is from the West. Know that you are loved. Receive this love and know you are God's son or daughter.

Now you can take your mind off you and keep your mind on the Father and His love. Life is going to be more meaningful for you, because when you receive God's love, you will be able to love others. You will become thankful, joyful, and peaceful, knowing your worth is based on the blood of Jesus Christ. You would realize you are worth the life of Jesus. You will rest in God's love. There will be an end to your struggle for acceptance, because you are forever accepted and approved by our loving Father.

> According as he hath chosen us in him before the foundation of the world, that we should be holy and without blame before him in love. (Ephesians 1:4)

> For by one offering he hath perfected forever them that are sanctified. (Hebrews 10:14)

Prayers and Declarations

It does not matter how deep you are in depression; you are walking out! In the name of Jesus, you are going to live and live well! Your future is bright! You have a living hope inside you! Christ in you is the hope of glory! You will come forth as pure gold! Your life is hidden in Christ, and Christ in God! You will live and eat the good of the land! Your past does not determine your future! In Christ, old things are passed away and all things are made new!

Your story is going to end well! All you need to do is decide in your heart that you will not give up, and hold tightly to the promise of soundness of mind. You have the final say. It is in your court. Take a decision to lay hold of what Christ did on the cross and not accept anything less. The enemy will flee.

Do you see the words I have declared above? Every single one of them applies to you as a child of God. Start declaring the Word of God out loud to yourself. Right now, you have to embrace the truth of God's Word to break free. The Word of God is truth. Settle it in your heart that you are going to believe God's Word above every feeling you experience. The Word says you have not been given the spirit of fear but the spirit of power, of love, and of a calm and well-balanced mind (2 Timothy 1:7).

Jesus said that His sheep hear His voice, they know Him, and they will not follow the voice of a stranger. Get acquainted with the written word so you can recognize the Father's voice when you hear it. Do not believe any loud thought telling you that you are worthless or that you are a failure or that you will never make it, or even telling you to kill yourself or that you are guilty. *Lies! Lies! Lies!* The Father says you are worth His life! Your path shines brighter and brighter. You will never be put to shame! Ecclesiastes 9:4 (KJV) says; "But for him who is joined to all the living, there is hope".

Never Alone

Now that you are a child of God, I want you to know that you are never going to be alone again. The Holy Spirit now lives in you and is ever present to guide you. He will comfort you, teach you, hold your hand, and lead you. Yes, He will discipline you, and yes, He will love on you. God is your Father, and He is a good Father. This is for all times. He will never turn His back on you. Speak to Him. Be assured by His presence and go forward in life confidently with Him. God is in you and God is for you. Cultivate the habit of spending time with God. Get a Bible you can understand, read it, and ask the Holy Spirit questions when you need understanding. Get ready for an exciting journey ahead. You are going to be living the best days of your life!

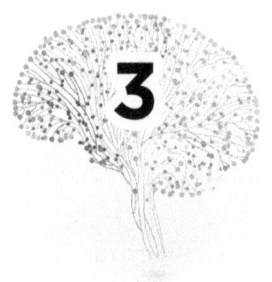

3

WHAT DEPRESSION REALLY IS

According to the *American Psychiatric Association's Diagnostic and Statistical Manual of Mental Disorders* (*DSM-5*), depression is defined by the presence of at least five out of a possible nine defining symptoms, present for at least two weeks, of sufficient severity to cause significant distress or impairment in social, occupational, or other important areas of functioning. These symptoms include the following:

1. Depressed mood most of the day, nearly every day
2. Markedly diminished interest or pleasure in all, or almost all, activities most of the day, nearly every day
3. Significant weight loss when not dieting, or weight gain, or a decrease or increase in appetite nearly every day
4. A slowing down of thought and a reduction of physical movement (observable by others, not merely subjective feelings of restlessness or being slowed down)
5. Fatigue or loss of energy nearly every day
6. Feelings of worthlessness or excessive or inappropriate guilt nearly every day
7. Diminished ability to think or concentrate, or indecisiveness, nearly every day

8. Recurrent thoughts of death, recurrent suicidal ideation without a specific plan, or a suicide attempt or a specific plan for committing suicide.

Depression can be classified as mild, moderate, or severe; such classification is determined by both the number and severity of symptoms, the persistence of other symptoms, and the degree of functional and social impairment.

The Cause of Depression

It is documented in medical texts that *the cause of depression is unknown*. There is, however, the school of thought that it is likely due to a complex interaction between biological, psychological, and social factors. A number of factors have been identified as triggers (e.g. having a chronic illness, use of medications, major life-changing events).

A Biblical View on What Really Causes Depression

Depression is not just about feeling transiently sad for a few days, as mentioned above. When you are depressed, you have a persistent feeling of sadness, loss of pleasure in previously enjoyed activities, and a range of other symptoms in varying degrees, including feeling hopeless, helpless, indecisive, and anxious; having poor self-esteem; and having suicidal thoughts and other thoughts that you realize you cannot just shake off.

While there may be a number of triggers for slipping into severe depression, it is important to know that *humanity has an enemy* who capitalizes on the events of life and predisposing factors to cause and perpetuate the heaviness and other symptoms experienced, by clouding our perspectives with the negativity that drives depression.

For example, if an individual goes through a life event such as the loss of a loved one or traumatic abuse, that individual's response to this event occurring would be determined by his or her mindset and belief systems, and what the individual holds to be true. The individual could either be filled with a sense of hopelessness, despair, discouragement, or worthlessness based on the perspective he or she holds about what is happening, or the individual could respond with courage, hope, expectation of healing, and, ultimately, restoration. This is where the individual's access to light, truth, and God matters, as well as his or her ability to yield to what He says. It is at this stage that the enemy capitalizes on the situation to provide perspectives that instil despair, despondency, and, ultimately, depression.

There are other factors that can make an individual more susceptible to the influence of the enemy and the overall effect of living in a fallen world. Some examples are the abuse of medications like steroids, some contraceptive pills, street drugs, and alcohol, as well as brain trauma. The good news is that God's Word can cure the effects of all these things.

Ultimately it all comes down to our thoughts and perspectives, and to the influence these have on our emotions.

Thoughts and Feelings

You will read and hear a lot about depression, but speaking from what I know as a Christian, someone who has experienced this, and as a doctor who sees patients every now and then with depression, I can tell you that what is felt as heaviness during a phase of depression is directly linked to what we are focused on in our minds. There are two key things that are helpful to know about getting free from depression. The first is that your thought patterns determine and control your feelings, and not the other way round. This is so key and is an underlying principle for getting free from the hold of depression. I speak more about the physical aspect of this in chapter 21 on a medical perspective, but I'll mention here that it is understood that when we think positive, happy thoughts, we stimulate the production of feel-good hormones, such as dopamine and serotonin. Negative thoughts reduce the production of these hormones. This is how antidepressants work—by boosting the presence and activity of some of these hormones. You can improve your mood by thinking positive thoughts.

When a person is in a state of depression, his or her thought patterns have become toxic; a massive web of negativity has been created, which is felt as the heaviness he or she is experiencing. The negative thoughts create a perspective on life that is dark and untrue, which clouds the mind in such a way that the individual would need the light and truth of God's love and His Word to bring clarity to his or her mind.

My prayer for you is that if you are in a state of depression right now, as you read this book you will see the light that I saw and you will be completely free.

The second thing to understand is that these negative thought patterns are instigated by the enemy and that, over time, the extent to which you yield yourself to these patterns of thinking is the extent to which he gets a hold of you and causes the terrible darkness and heaviness of depression. "To appoint unto them that mourn in Zion, to give unto them beauty for ashes, the oil of joy for mourning, the garment of praise for the spirit of heaviness; that they might be called trees of righteousness, the planting of the Lord, that he might be glorified" (Isaiah 61:3 KJV).

We can draw the following conclusions from the two points made above:

1. A spirit of heaviness is at the root cause of depression, with a physical expression seen as a change in hormones and other symptoms.
2. The battle is fought in our minds.

There are many reasons why a person may become depressed, but I would like to share with you common triggers I have identified from my life and the things I see affecting other people. They are the common denominators I see as the core issues underlying most causes of depression.

The Triggers of Depression

Common triggers that tip people into being depressed are a poor self-image, fear, anxiety and worry, failure, disappointment, guilt, regret, indecision and confusion, hurt, and grief. These pitfalls result in loss of one's peace and joy and make one find it difficult to ever see oneself getting beyond the situation. This picture of gloom grows large in one's mind and makes one feel as if one's world is over. Permit me to address each of these issues in this book and say to you what I know the Father wants you to know.

The Human Makeup

Before we go on, I need you to understand a bit of the structure of our makeup as described by the scriptures. I need you to understand that the human being is a spirit; he has a soul, which is made up of his mind, will, and emotions, and he lives in a body. 1 Thessalonians 5:23 describes us as spirit, soul, and body. The feelings we have are controlled by the thoughts in our minds. The mind is where the battle is won or lost. You can win this battle once you gain the control of your thoughts and replace the negative thought patterns you have. When this happens, you will then be able to navigate your way out of the web of negativity that is causing the heaviness in your heart. Understanding this will transform your experience of darkness to joy. The unravelling of these webs of thoughts is accomplished only by thoughts inspired by the light of the truth of God's Word.

Unravelling the Negative Thought Patterns

Throughout this book I would like to encourage you to apply a system God taught me, with which you can unravel the negative thought patterns that perpetuate the heaviness of depression—and not just that, but a system that can be used to reprogramme minds for success with His Word.

Psychologists call the negative thoughts that perpetuate the negative emotions of depression "hot thoughts".

We will be using God's Word to unravel these hot thoughts, these lies, these negative perspectives. We will be shining light over our minds and therefore causing changes that will disarm the darkness and produce results in our minds and brains, causing healing, restoration, and joy to be felt within our entire beings.

The System for Healing and Restoring the Mind with God's Word

- **Behold** the Word. (Keep it in your vision, write it, use it as a screen saver, put up images, read it, and visualize it.)
- **Believe** the Word (at a heart level; truly believe, and show this in action).
- **Think** the Word. (Ponder and contemplate it.)
- **Speak** the Word (Declare it, affirm it, and bring it into your language of expression.)
- **Become** what the Word says.

For every *truth* you receive in this book at the end of each chapter, I encourage you to intentionally daily take out time to *behold* (focus, visualize, and imagine) the truth you have embraced, *believe* it (at a heart level, proven by action), *think about* it (ponder, reflect, contemplate), *speak* it (affirm it, declare it, and get into your language of expression), and watch yourself *become what it says*.

Please do this for at least twenty-one days, because it takes an average of twenty-one days to build long-term memory.

Long-term memory refers to our having taken new information within us and built effective and useful memory networks formed by neurons that can release the signals that can cause change within us and produce lasting healing and restorative, transformative results.

As we do this practical exercise daily, we will essentially be rewiring our brains with truth.

We will be healing and renewing our thinking. As you think on the truth of God's Word, new neuronal pathways with healthy, life-giving information will be created to allow for signals that will transmit the required chemicals to make you whole and restored.

I can assure you that if you give your mind wholly to the truth over your experience, you will be free. "And ye shall know the truth, and the truth shall make you free" (John 8:32).

I have shared my personal story with you, but I acknowledge that some people may be depressed or feel hopeless and may not have come to this point of depression the same way I did. Some people may have gone through a devastating life experience causing grief, or they may have been abused or may have experienced failure, disappointment, heartache—the list can go on and on. But regardless of the trigger, the enemy's strategy is the same; he lies to you and pushes you into the depths of depression and hopelessness, which feels the same for all and is no place for anyone to remain. God definitely doesn't want you there. He wants you free and full of joy!

Christ's finished work on the cross will deliver anyone and set anyone free, regardless of what has brought them down into the depths of depression, and will restore their joy, peace, and whatever was lost. You are never beyond the love of the Father. You are not just coming out of depression; you are already out by the finished works of Jesus Christ, and all I am going to do is show you this truth with the help of the Holy Spirit so you can walk free!

4

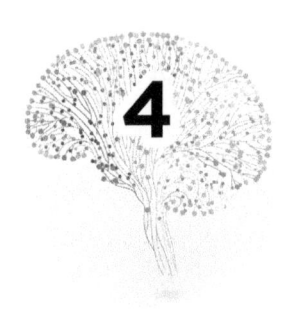

FREEDOM FROM A POOR SELF-IMAGE

Self-image is an area I struggled with in my life. I had such a poor image of myself. I just never felt good enough. I was very critical of myself, and I was very self-absorbed. I did not really know who I was as God's child. I am so grateful that as I look into God's Word daily, I can now see who I am clearly. I am God's beloved and the apple of His eye!

Do you know that you are God's son or daughter? Think about that for a while. Let that thought begin to change whatever perception you have of yourself. You are of extreme value. Jesus had you in His mind when He was going to the cross; you were one of the people He was thinking about. The scriptures say, "For the joy set before Him, He endured the cross and He despised the shame." You were the joy set before Him. "Looking unto Jesus the author and finisher of our faith; who for the joy that was set before him endured the cross, despising the shame, and is set down at the right hand of the throne of God." (Hebrews 12:2 KJV).

Let me paint a true picture of you for you. When Jesus went to the cross, you died with Him; the life you now live, you live by Him. The old you is gone. You have a brand-new life and identity in Christ, and it is one of royalty. You are loved, and you have been created anew in Christ. The Bible says you are God's workmanship: "For we are his workmanship, created in Christ Jesus for good works, which God prepared beforehand, that we should walk in them" (Ephesians 2:10 KJV).

Workmanship refers to the degree of skill with which a product is made or a job is done. You are a show-off of the degree of skill with which God creates. Isn't that an amazing thought? You are one of a kind. You ought to be comfortable and pleased with you. You are a piece of art—a masterpiece, actually. Only you can be you, the way you are. You are unique, distinct, gifted, and of great value. Only you can smile the way you do. Only you can talk the way you do. Your mannerisms and your features are so special. Nobody else on the planet has ever been like you or will ever be like you. This is the picture of the amazing work of an amazing God. You are an expression of the beauty and glory of the Father. You are His kid, so you should expect nothing less.

This new life you have since you got born again is hidden in Christ, and Christ in God. You can boldly say out loud, "In Christ I am of great value! I am worth the blood of Christ! I am valuable not in my capacity or my ability, but because Jesus loves me and nothing shall be able to separate me from the love of Christ! Therein lies my value. I am valuable because I am loved. I have been chosen, even before the world began. I have been accepted and approved, and this has nothing to do with anything I have done, except for God's decision to love me and value me because He was pleased to."

The value of a thing is determined by what a person is willing to pay for it. God chose to pay for you with the blood of His Son. Wow!

That says a lot about how valuable you are. Please choose to know and believe the Father's love.

In yourself, you would never have been good enough. In yourself, you were not perfect, and you would never have been. If the enemy attacked your mind with thoughts of worthlessness, he would win if you tried to defend yourself with just your qualities. There would always be something about you that was not good enough. You would be guilty as charged. But guess what? When that thought comes, you can respond boldly by saying, It's not about me at all. The old me died with Christ, and now Christ lives here. I am a daughter [or son], I am royalty, and I've got birthrights. I am free, I am perfect in Christ, I am the righteousness of God, I am an heir of God, and I am a bona fide daughter [or son] of the living God!"

When you approach things this way, the enemy will have nothing on you. You'll beat him hands down. You'll soar with wings because nothing can stop you now. You are at the core of your identity. Awesome!

Do you know that if you even tried to look into all the good you think you have to make yourself feel better about yourself, that would only make you prideful? Some people get to a point of so much worthlessness and self-hate because the enemy lies so much to them and they believe every lie, such that they then go on to harm themselves and inflict pain and hurt on themselves. This leads to self-cutting and all sorts of means of causing pain. The lies become so great that for some, it is a way to relieve the pressure inflicted by the enemy, like the man at the tomb who cried and cried and cut himself with stones (Mark 5:5). The enemy oppresses the soul of such people. I see so many people like this in my practice who are hoping for medicine that will help. There is only so much that medical help can offer, but praise God for Jesus! When He steps in, darkness bows to Him!

She said, "I Am Fat and Ugly."

I once saw a lady who had a very terrible view of herself. She had used blades to inscribe on her thighs that she was fat and ugly. When she looked in the mirror, this was all she could see. My heart longed to be able to tell her otherwise.

A lot of people have all sorts of opinions of themselves, but in Christ, your view of you should start and end from within. This picture of you is then what reflects itself on the outside.

Seeing Who You Are in the Light of the Mirror of Truth

The real you is your spirit. You can see this part of you in the Word of God. The Word of God is light, and when the light steps in, darkness flees. How do you put on the light? By lighting your candle. Your spirit man is the candle of the Lord, and you light him with the light of the Word of God (Proverbs 20:27). You see, man is a spirit; he has a soul and lives in a body. His soul is his mind, will, and emotions. The spirit man gets born again when we receive Jesus. A recreation happens. When this happens, we immediately become a new creation. Old things pass away. Our inner man (the spirit), being the real man, is made anew in the perfect likeness of God in righteousness. We are perfected and sanctified forever. We died with Christ and were raised up with Him. As such, the life we now live, we live by the faith of the Son of God, who died for us and gave Himself up for us (Galatians 2:20). Therefore it is no longer me, but Christ in me. So everything He is, I am! Our minds then have to be renewed with the Word of God to this reality. This involves a change in mindset; this is even more so in the case of the battle against depression.

We look at the mirror of the Word and see who we are in Christ, and we boldly speak! We can now look at ourselves and say "praise God! I am perfect in Christ! I am the righteousness of God, I am the beloved of God and I am accepted in the beloved" (Ephesians 1:6). I can look at myself and see that. Wow! When God sees me, He sees Jesus and He says, "Let's put on her the best robe, the signet ring and shoes on her feet. Let's kill the fattest calf and have a party, for my daughter is home!" (Luke 15:22). I can see that I am the apple of God's eye. I can see He thinks about me 24/7 and His thoughts towards me are precious. They outnumber the grains of sand on the seashore (Psalm 139:17–18). Each one of those thoughts is a thought of good, to prosper me and not to harm me; to give me a future and an expected end (Jeremiah 29:11). I can say confidently that I am fearfully and wonderfully made (Psalm 139:14).

It is time to cast down every contrary imagination and take captive every contrary thought; bringing it into subjection to the Word of God (2 Corinthians 10:5). Therefore, when a thought comes and tells you something like "you are not worth anything", "kill yourself", or "you are worthless", you must say out loud—and I mean it when I say you must speak out loud—"No! I am worth the price of the blood of Jesus! I am loved by God!"

5

FREEDOM FROM FEAR, ANXIETY, AND WORRY

I know too well about that wave of utter dread called fear that tries to overcome your being. It tries to paint a picture that you are helpless and subject to its effect. I want to give you two amazing truths that will put an end to fear in your life.

First is the truth that perfect love will end fear. Perfect love is your Father. His love is absolute. When I realized in my heart that this love is without condition and I did not earn it and so cannot lose it, and that I am guaranteed this love always and at all times, peace and boldness surged in me. When I also realized what God will do for the one He loves and how much He loved me, knowing and believing this love made my faith in God's word for me skyrocket, and fear went out the door.

> There is no fear in love; but perfect love casteth out fear: because fear hath torment. He that feareth is not made perfect in love. (1 John 4:18)

> And we have known and believed the love that God hath to us. God is love; and he that dwelleth in love dwelleth in God, and God in him. (1 John 4:16)

Secondly, Christ is in you. It is Him against that fear; not you. As such, you are victorious already. Christ is greater! The greater one lives in you! (1 John 4:4). You can take refuge in your Father's love and open your mouth and demand fear to stop in its tracks. You have got to realize that fear is a spirit and you are not subject to it. As you rest in your Father's love and face what causes fear by speaking to it to make it leave, and as you take steps in the direction it has been intimidating you with, you will soon see that whatever it was will flee from you, and you'll be free!

You see, *perfect love casts out all fear!* When you get your mind fixed on the love of God and His word, He will keep you in perfect peace. God commands us to be anxious for nothing, but in all things by prayer and petition we are to make our requests known to Him; then His peace, which passes all understanding, will guard our hearts and minds in Christ (Philippians 4:6–7). He tells us to do only what He has given us the capacity to do.

What are you thinking about? You are to think thoughts that are true, admirable, and of good report. Ask yourself whether those thoughts are true. Those thoughts that come bringing fear are always lies. The Word of God always speaks peace. Remember that the battle is in the mind and it does not last always. The only truth is God's Word. Find what God's Word has to say about that thing that causes you fear, but most of all, get a revelation of God's love for you. For if the Father loves you, then nothing—absolutely nothing—can separate you from this love. What, then, is this thing that you fear?

Freedom from a Phobia

I remember that in the past, I had a phobia of closed spaces, which is called "claustrophobia." The first time I realized this was when my siblings and I were playing a game and it involved being locked in a cupboard from the outside. The idea was to see who could stay inside the longest. I realized I needed to get out quickly, and I became stricken with panic when my sister didn't open it up right away. This phobia almost impacted my ability to fly, travel by train, etc. There was one time back in Nigeria when I boarded a vehicle to travel to school. It was a bus, and it was being filled with luggage. A stack of boxes was being piled up high on my side. I asked the man setting up the bags to please rearrange them because I was already feeling confined. When he ignored me after multiple attempts to get him to respond, the fear took over, and I pushed everything on my side down and jumped out of the bus. Fortunately it wasn't moving yet. Now, what he did was not great, but no one should be under the impulsive control of fear, as I was. This phobia would manifest itself in many other ways for me on lifts, amusement park rides, and so on.

Praise Jesus, as I faced the thoughts that arose during these episodes and refused to give in to them, the enemy had to back down. My body began to respond less and less with a racing heartbeat, sweating, and so forth. When I decided I was not going to let the enemy have his way in this manner any more, I no longer ever described myself as someone who was claustrophobic. I dropped that label. I would sit still in those first moments of fighting the fear-driven impulses, fixed on the unshakable reality of the Word of God that He is with me. I would speak in tongues, acknowledge my Father's presence, smile, chat, and the like, even as I felt my heart pounding and my body telling me to scream. Sure enough, it was not long before the enemy did not bother me any more. He is a defeated foe, and we are born winners!

Let the love of God become so real to you that it will make everything else become irrelevant. Cast your cares upon Him, for He cares for you. Do not let your heart be troubled. Refuse to fear. Be still and know He is God. The palpitations you feel and the overwhelming sense of doom that comes upon you are mirages. These things are as real as you allow them to be. Go in the name of Jesus and face what it is the enemy is trying to scare you away from. The symptoms will dissipate. Remember: the enemy *will* flee (James 4:7).

You have not been given the spirit of fear. You are no longer a slave to fear. You have the spirit of sonship, and you can cry "Abba Father". You have straight access to the throne room. You dwell there. You are sitting down in heavenly realms in Christ. No one can snatch you from the Father. Even though you walk through the valley of the shadow of death, fear no evil, for He is not just with you, but in you.

Never identify yourself as a fearful person. Avoid expressing yourself with fear-related words. Do not say to yourself, "my anxiety", "my fears", or "my dread". If the Father says He has not given you a spirit of fear, then it means fear of any sort is not coming out from you but is foreign to you and comes as an imposter and must be resisted till it flees. Don't embrace fear. Jesus said so often, "fear not". See this as words of comfort but also as a command. To win and live the life Jesus paid for us to have, we must not tolerate fear.

Freedom from Worry

I have now learnt that it is not OK to just embrace fear, worry, and anxiety. The trick of worry is subtle, because by embracing fear, worry, or anxiety, you think you are being responsible about issues. It took me a while to realize this wasn't the case. I felt I needed to worry about anything I felt was not in place or under my control. We were not built to carry the burden of worry. It is an illusion to think that by worrying we make anything better.

Jesus said something that makes me laugh at myself these days if I find myself about to slip into worry. Jesus said we cannot even make ourselves taller by worrying. So what's the point? Ha! "And which of you with taking thought can add to his stature one cubit? If ye then be not able to do that thing which is least, why take ye thought for the rest?" (Luke 12:25–26 KJV).

I remind myself about a couple of other things like "Hey Nkiru, the earth is rotating on its axis and we are revolving round the sun. Your heart is beating, and so much is going on that is outside of your control. So just relax in God and His word." I love what 1 Peter 5:7 says: "Casting all your care upon him; for he careth for you."

Do you know that those thoughts that come at you triggering worry and fear are fiery darts of the enemy (Ephesians 6:16)? Do you know what we do with fiery darts? We block them with the shield of faith. The weapons of our warfare are described in Ephesians 6. Have a look at all of them. If perfect love casts out all fear, then raise up the shield of faith in the unending love of God. He says that nothing shall be able to separate you from His love.

Romans 8:37–39 states, "Nay in all these things, we are more than conquerors through him that loved us. For I am persuaded, that neither death nor life, nor angels, nor principalities, nor powers, nor things present, nor things to come, nor height, nor depth, nor any creature, shall be able to separate us from the love of God, which is in Christ Jesus our Lord."

Wow! Do you see that? You cannot outdo or outrun the love of God. David said, "Where can I go from your presence, if I ascend into heaven you are there, If I lay my bed in hell, behold thou art there" (Psalm 139:8).

Try saying this out loud right now: "God loves me! God loves me! God loves me! I refuse to fear! Yes!"

Listen to Daddy, Not a stranger

As I encourage you to be rooted in God's love and tell fear to get away, I must echo some important truths about fear. Fear is not OK. Before I do go on to share what I am about to share, I want you to know that if you feel fear, it is no condemnation to you at all. I have felt fear in many ways; it has been significant enough to affect my sleep and make me feel extremely terrified, but what I am trying to pass on is a perspective that says, "Wait a minute; this isn't right. I am not going to put up with this any more"—a perspective to dare to say, "Father God, I'm so sorry I have allowed myself to listen to the enemy for so long. Forgive me; I know I can't do this on my own, but I trust you and I know you are here to help, and I'm ready to resist fear in the name of Jesus.

I was shocked to see the way scriptures describe fear. In the book of Revelation 21:8, the fearful are put in a group that you would be shocked to note. Praise God, we are not going to be judged based on our actions but based on what Christ has done and our faith in His blood that makes us right with God, but this clearly shows us that to live in fear is not right at all. We have got to resist fear with hearts rooted in the love of God and faith in what our Father has to say.

I thought to myself, "How is it that the fearful are seen this way?" Then I realized that fear can be described as the result of having more faith in what the Devil says than in what God says. Imagine you have a child and you keep telling him or her words of comfort, admonishing the child not to fear, yet that child chooses to give in to the words of a stranger saying they will hurt the child, and chooses to believe those words over your words. You would definitely feel unhappy with your child about this. I am in no way discounting the feeling of fear you experience, but I am showing you that it is to be resisted and not embraced.

What you believe, you empower. Therefore, if you believe the Devil, you empower him, because you end up releasing faith in his lies. Once you begin to speak those lies, you literally give life to those things he has presented to you.

Fighting Fear

It is not enough to just hold up the shield of faith and defend. You do need to strike back with the sword of the Spirit. This is the spoken Word of God (Hebrews 4:12). To fight the good fight of faith, you do need to keep your eyes and your ears constantly receiving the Word of God in your heart, and then you *speak it out loud* with conviction. When you have that sense of anxiety or worry come at you, say "I will not let my heart be troubled", "my Father cares for me", "the hairs on my head are all numbered", "Father God calls me by name", "the Father loves me with an everlasting love", "all things are working together for my good", "I have peace that passes all understanding", "light rises in the darkness for me", and "I will not be agitated, for I have self-control!" Go through the scriptures and meditate on them. These words in your heart and in your mouth will set you free. You will know the truth, and the truth will set you free if you continue in the Word.

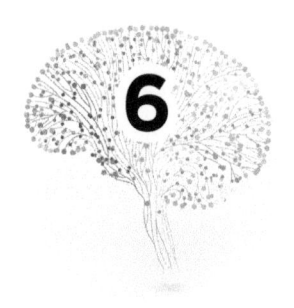

FREEDOM FROM FAILURE

One of the questions I have to ask my patients when assessing them for depression is whether they feel like they are failures and that they have let themselves or their families down. It is one of many questions on a questionnaire called the PHQ 9, which is used for assessing severity of depression. Most of the time, my patients break down in tears at this point, and I listen to them tell me why they feel like failures. Lots of people do feel this way. Do you feel this way? You do not have to.

There are two issues here. Some people feel like failures as a whole. They see themselves as failures, while some others cannot get over a specific perceived failure from the past. In my past, I tended to define myself by my inefficiencies or perceived failures. This is one reason why I did my best to succeed. I gained affirmation from my ability to perform. I was a perfectionist, and the thought of failing at something would cause me so much distress because I connected my actions and results with my identity. Now I am free, and you can be too.

If you feel like a failure, what is happening is that you are defining yourself based on your actions and results. Your actions do not define who you are. To call yourself a failure is to undermine who God made you as. Even if you slip, the Bible says the righteous man may fall seven times but will still get up (Proverbs 24:16a). The fact that he falls does not have any effect on his righteousness. This means that in God's sight, you are not your mistakes. You are still His beloved child who has the inherent capacity to succeed, because He already calls you a success. You see, in the kingdom, when we make a perceived mistake, we acknowledge what we did, we talk to God about it, we receive grace and mercy, and we learn from it and move on to greater things with God. We do not carry the burden of shame, guilt, or condemnation. Jesus bore it all already.

This is explained well in 2 Corinthians 7:10: "For godly sorrow worketh repentance to salvation not to be repented of: but the sorrow of the world worketh death."

"Repentance" here speaks of a mindset change—a learning that occurs following acknowledgement of the issue and leaves you better rather than taking on the weight of guilt, shame, or condemnation, which is what the death spoken of refers to. No matter what it is we did, God holds no grudges with us. Once a son, always a son, as long as we continue to look to the blood of Jesus, which is enough and sufficient.

I am not here to try to convince you that your past mistakes did not happen, but I am here to tell you that in Christ *old things are passed away*. Actually, in Christ the past is gone. The past has no say over your today and tomorrow. You can look at whatever you did or didn't do in the past that tries to weigh you down and say to yourself, "I may have slipped, but now I have a new slate because of Christ. That was my past." You can say, "I will embrace my today with hope and expectations, because I am who God says I am. I am A *success* by His standards. I am undefeated by His rules, because He has succeeded for me. He is God, and who He says I am is who I am."

Today can be the beginning of embracing the truth that God does not see your past and does not see you as a failure. Raise your head up high, for in Christ there is no more shame (Isaiah 61:7) or condemnation or guilt (Romans 8:1).

Isaiah 61:7 states, "For your shame ye shall have double; and for confusion they shall rejoice in their portion: therefore in their land they shall possess the double: everlasting joy shall be unto them."

God knows the depth of what you consider your failure. He knows you messed up, but He sees who you are now and He sees who you can be. He does not want you wallowing in the mud of defeat. He is saying to you, "Awake, awake; put on your strength, put on your beautiful garments, shake yourself from the dust, arise and sit down" (Isaiah 52:1–2, paraphrased). Let me show you how the Father treats the perceived failures of his children.

The Prodigal Son (Luke 15)

A son walked away from his father, who was the description of our heavenly Father. He went out into the world and messed up big time. His life was dirty and dark. All he could do was muster the courage to come back to his father and possibly be a servant, because of the shame and guilt that he had. When he came back—my goodness—the father *ran to him!* The father immediately acknowledged him as his son, placed on him the best robe, gave him a signet ring, and put shoes on his feet. He did not let him say one word about not deserving to be a son or deserving to be a servant. The father rejoiced that *his son* was back. Praise God! When we come to Him, He *does not regard the past*, and He does not stop there. He reinstates us and shows us off. He will throw a party for you. He will restore the years lost.

Peter

Peter knew the Lord Jesus. Peter had been with Him all those three years, and at the end, Peter denied Him three times. My goodness! He could have hidden his head in the mud and told himself he was an outright failure. He had let Jesus down. He could have said, "I'll never amount to anything. I am such a loser. I deserve to die." He could have gone ahead and killed himself. You might say here that I am probably pushing it too far, but no, I am not. Someone else did just that. Judas did that. Judas betrayed Jesus, could not handle the guilt and shame, and killed himself. How unfortunate. God is no respecter of persons. He will not turn anyone away who comes to Him, regardless of what that person has done. If Judas recognized this and turned to God, he would have received grace and mercy. Thank God He is a master of completely transforming the life of any person who gives Him the chance. Peter received grace and mercy and became the bold minister and apostle of God that he was.

Forget the past and press on to the future. There is a great tomorrow ahead for you. The Father does not condemn you. He makes all things beautiful in His time. You can start now to walk with Him to correct whatever needs to be corrected. And even if anything has to be recreated, He can do so! *Nothing is impossible with God!*

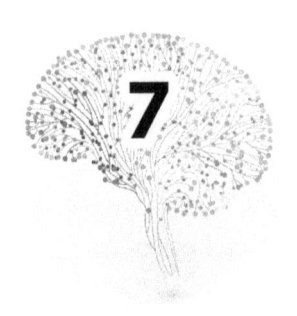

FREEDOM FROM DISAPPOINTMENT

When things do not go as we hoped, and when plans we set out do not seem to have worked out the way we expected them to, there can be a huge sense of dismay and disappointment. Now, while there will be the initial wave of emotions stirred up when things do not go as planned, do you know that we do not have to dwell there? I appreciate that it might feel easier to just accommodate those feelings and feel terrible, but hey, we don't have to remain stuck there. We have the ability to turn away from all that's happened and look up to God. When we do this, we can gain perspective from Him that will set us above what has happened.

Those first few moments when you realize things have not gone according to plan are so key in terms of your response. Come away, shut the door to your room, pour out your heart to God, and let His love and His presence shine through. Then go voraciously for His words. You will be set up to surf the waves and come to dry ground and not get swallowed up.

A key perspective that will always be true regardless of what has happened is that Romans 8:28 says all things work together for good to them that love God and are called according to His purpose. Another key perspective is that no matter what has happened to you in your journey of life, if you are reading this, it means you are alive, and that counts for a lot. You might be thinking, "Well, it's no good being alive, because life does not seem to be making any sense to me." Is it OK if I let you know that is not true? Here is what truth says: "For to him that is joined to all the living there is hope: for a living dog is better than a dead lion" (Ecclesiastes 9:4).

If you are alive, you have hope! If you are alive, you are still in the race. If you are alive, God still has great plans for you for your time on earth.

I remember when it looked like my whole life was falling apart. During this season of fighting for life, I had to step out of medical school, and I was told I may not be able to go back. I was told it might be difficult for me. They said it was probably going to put me under a lot of stress. I remember creating a fixed picture of myself as a medical doctor. I was not going to let that shift. I would respond to the thought by saying "I might never make it," looking at that picture I had created in my mind. I said to myself, "I am going to make it. I am going to succeed." My confidence hinged on an anchor I had set on God's love and His word. I always remember when I said to Him, "Daddy, you love me too much to let me fail. You love me too much for this to be the end of my life. You love me too much for me to end this way. No! You love me! I believe your love! I will have a beautiful life." So I hung on to that word while swimming through the waves, and praise God, I began to surf on the waves and got to dry ground! It may not feel easy, but if you dare to hold on, you will be in awe at what your future will be. It is vitally important to stay expectant.

Be Expectant

It is important to wake up and be expectant. Be expectant for the day, for the week, for the month, for the year, and for your life! Say to yourself, "It's going to be a great day!"

It is important to think about your future and be expectant. It sends a message of joyful motivation to your whole being. At every point in time, look forward to something. Don't look backwards except to remember and be thankful. Look ahead always, and *look up!*

Set your mind on things above (Colossians 3:2–10). Set your mind on God's sure promises! Set your mind on God's everlasting love for you. Be convinced and fully persuaded that His goodness is for you in this life.

Say, like David, "I will see God's goodness in the land of the living! Goodness and mercies are following me daily!"

David said that if he had not believed, he would not have seen the goodness of the Lord in the land of the living (Psalm 27:13). Thank God he believed and he saw! Let that be your story too.

Don't you dare give up! Don't just go through the motions.

Live it up! Live excited! Live expectant!

The promises are sure! Wait for them. They shall not tarry! They will speak and not lie! (Habakkuk 2:3). You have got to constantly remind yourself that regardless of what has happened, God is able to make it work together for your good. "And we know that all things work together for good to them that love God, to them who are the called according to his purpose" (Romans 8:28).

Do not think that God is against you. Remember: every good and perfect gift comes from Him (James 1:17). This does not stop Him from turning around what the enemy wanted to use to harm you, for your good. Do not be dismayed or discouraged. It is never too late; it is never so broken. It is never over unless you decide it is. You have in you His Spirit. You are more than a conqueror through Christ who loves you. This season will pass. Keep steady and hold on. Just rest in God's promises. "Fear thou not; for I *am* with thee: be not dismayed; for I *am* thy God: I will strengthen thee; yea, I will help thee; yea, I will uphold thee with the right hand of my righteousness" (Isaiah 41:10 KJV).

Keep hope alive. Hope maketh not ashamed: "And hope maketh not ashamed; because the love of God is shed abroad in our hearts by the Holy Ghost which is given unto us" (Romans 5:5).

Say to yourself, as David says in Psalm 43:5, "Why art thou cast down, O my soul? And why art thou disquieted within me? Hope in God: for I shall yet praise him, *who is* the health of my countenance, and my God."

Action: Write out scripture-based promises for the future and place them on your wall. Put them on your screensavers and paste pictures relating to them around you, giving you a clear picture of what it is you can look forward to. See them every day, and thank God for them, because they will come to pass.

8

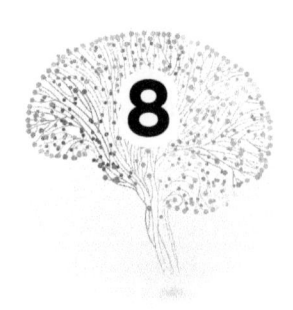

FREEDOM FROM GUILT

Guilt can be a pitfall leading to depression and can also be one of the terrible feelings experienced during a depressive episode. I remember feeling so guilty at some point during my downturn. All of a sudden, all my shortcomings became so magnified. You see, the enemy attacks the mind of the depressed person by emphasizing everything negative. This is why he is called the accuser of the brethren. How do you get past your wrongdoing? What if you are actually guilty according to the facts? What if you did what he said you did? What if, by the world's standards, you should legitimately be accused? If that were all there was to it, what a terrible situation it would be to live under the condemnation of your wrongdoing.

The enemy points fingers at you and reminds you of your misdeeds. He knows that if he can get you to live in condemnation, you will never be able to believe and receive all that the Father has for you. If you remain tuned in to what he says, he'll strip you of all your peace, joy, and hope and keep you down and depressed. You will never be free. There are consequences for the wrong done, but praise God the story does not end there!

I remember speaking to a man who was struggling with depression, and he told me he was finding it difficult to get over some wrong things he had done in the past that caused him a lot of shame. Medically, there was no answer for him. I knew the only answer would be for him to know that Jesus had paid for his guilt. In the setting I was in, I could not share this, but I believe there are lots of people reading this book who need to receive forgiveness and forgive themselves to allow for joy.

The Bible says in the book of Romans 8:33–34 (KJV), "Who shall lay anything to the charge of God's elect? It is God that justifieth. Who is he that condemneth? It is Christ that died, yea rather, that is risen again, who is even at the right hand of God, who also maketh intercession for us."

Wow! What a load of fresh air. You are free. Your punishment has been paid for by another person. Yes, you were supposed to pay for your wrongdoing, but now you have been acquitted. You do not have to feel bad any more, but just be thankful and full of joy. You are justified. God loves you and has approved of you. Your guilt was carried by Jesus, and when He died, it went away. Now He is risen and has given you a new life in Him. All your debt has been paid. Do not feel guilty one more day. Receive His love and live.

The penalty for sin is death, but the gift of God is eternal life! Praise God! We have been given the gift of righteousness. This is God's nature—God's rightness. We did not earn it. It was a gift we received. The due punishment for our wrongdoing, no matter what it was, has been served. Jesus took our place and has paid the price forever. We stand holy and blameless before God in love (Ephesians 1:4). We are accepted in the beloved of the Father. There is therefore now no condemnation to those who are in Christ Jesus. You can respond to the accusation by saying out loud, "I am righteous! I am accepted!"

Galatians 2:20 says I was crucified with Christ and I no longer live, but Christ lives in me. The old man is gone. We have been created anew in Christ Jesus. Once you get a hold of this truth, do not let it go. Very soon the enemy will not have anything on you. The Bible says Jesus perfected us forever (Hebrews 10:14). This is why we can come boldly to the throne of grace. We can run confidently into our Father's arms without one iota of feeling condemned or impure, because we are perfect in His eyes. We are His righteousness. We are His children born of the same life that He has. Isn't this amazing?

Forget the former things and look unto the beauty that God has made you become. You are justified—and now glorified. He sees everything you were, and He holds nothing against you. The full payment has been completed in Christ. You are holy and accepted by God (Ephesians 1). Now you have the ability to walk in the abundance of grace He has given you to live above sin and walk in the fruits of righteousness. And I will also say that even though you may appear to fall again, do not run away from God, but run closer to Him. Say you are sorry, rise up, and plead the blood of Jesus. Do not plead guilty. Repent of that thing. Receive wisdom, learn, receive grace, and walk on, strong and at peace with God.

Free of Guilt Day to Day

I have learnt to live day to day free from guilt. Let me give you a picture of what I mean. In the past, I would feel so bad with myself for making a mistake, saying something inappropriate or just anything that I felt I shouldn't have done. This would then lead to thoughts like "Nkiru, you always do this, you are just like this." It was so much pressure. It made me so defensive. This would obviously cast a shadow over me, and for a period I would be feeling unhappy with myself.

Now, a different way I approach anything I do or say that may not be appropriate is that I am able to acknowledge this. I see that I'm on a journey, that I'm not perfect in myself but in Jesus and because of Him, and that I do not need to carry the burden of guilt or shame. All I do is turn to Father God, ask for help, receive what it takes to be better, and in love make whatever amends need to be made. I do all this while remaining at peace with myself and full of joy, knowing God loves me.

It may not always be so intense, but at all times, if the enemy comes at you with thoughts of condemnation, do not accept them. When you do something that's not OK, it's important to acknowledge this. Talk to God. Tell Him you're sorry. Receive grace and empowerment not to continue in that thing. Renew your mind with the word of God in that area of life, but never wallow in shame. You are a son or daughter. Ask the prodigal son in Luke 15:11. Even if you almost ate pig food, you remain God's son or daughter, and He'll always love you and bless you.

Godly sorrow leads to repentance, and the world's sorrow leads to death (2 Corinthians 7:10). Be like Peter and not Judas. Don't take the burden that Jesus bore for you. He bore your guilt, and He bore your shame. Walk free! You should acknowledge a mistake, learn from it, and grow, but you do not have to carry the guilt or shame tied to it, because Jesus has already done this. This is what 2 Corinthians 7:10 above means. Godly sorrow leads to a changed person, not a guilt-ridden and condemned person. Your identity remains intact. You will always be a son or a daughter of God.

I'll just stop here to pray that you understand all I am saying. I ask that light will flood your heart and you will see clearly who you are right now. I declare that every lie of the enemy being thrown at you, sowing seeds of condemnation, will *stop now* in the name of Jesus! You are God's workmanship created in Christ anew unto good works that He planned before the foundation of the world. Nothing and no one can stop this.

9

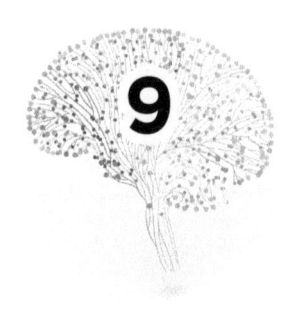

FREEDOM FROM REGRET

Anything that keeps your mind stuck, causing you to be unable to look forward with joyful expectation, is a pitfall leading to depression. Regret is one of those things. It can be such an intense source of heaviness for a person who constantly plays over and over in his or her mind something that happened in the past which the person wishes he or she could have changed. The person keeps going into the past, reactivating the thoughts surrounding the event and trying to work out the different ways he or she could have prevented it from happening. It can hurt, and the hurt can be perpetuated as the thoughts play on. Some people have to live with a physical representation, such as a scar or an objective reminder of what happened.

When I Cut My Son's Hair

I want to share a story about when I cut my son's hair and some things I learnt about regret. I know this will not even compare with some stories some of you will have, but I am sharing this only to help paint a picture of hope that only the Holy Spirit can paint.

My son Fijinoluwa had always had lots of hair, and even when we cut it, we didn't cut it low. He was about 2 years old when I suddenly felt I should get him to have a haircut. I took him to the barber, where we had a very distressing experience cutting his hair! He screamed and cried all through it. The barber found it difficult to cut his hair the way he wanted to. We were left there with my son having what looked like a skin cut with no borders. I practically wanted to cry because I couldn't recognize who he was! Ha, ha, ha! My cute little son with lots of hair looked so different. When I got home, his dad was stunned, as was his nanny. He honestly looked weird. I cried because I now had to live with this decision I had made.

As I lay on my bed, talking to God about how upset I was with myself for cutting my son's hair this way, I felt a twinge of regret come over me. I started thinking about how I could have prevented this. I found myself thinking about how great he had looked with his hair before we went out. Why I had even wanted to cut his hair I didn't know.

As I dwelt on these thoughts, I found myself feeling sad. Then I became alert about what was going on in my mind. I realized that even though this may have seemed trivial, I had to respond to these thoughts causing regret. Although looking at him was constantly reminding me of my decision, I had the truth to focus on, which was that hair grows back! Sure enough, his hair did grow again!

"But Nkiru, that was simple," you may say. You may say that was easy to get past, and I agree with you, but taking the principles from that story, there is always the truth, which is the equivalent of "hair grows back" in God's Word. There is always a definite, sure word that will inspire peace, hope, and courage over whatever you are facing. Reach for it, hold on to it, don't let it out of your sight, and it will be only a matter of time before your current experience is taken over by this truth.

I know regret can hurt, but praise God it doesn't have to drown you. If you are God's child, do you know that no matter what has happened in the past, there is a *guaranteed* brighter future for you? This is the game changer for you. Outside of God, it is hit and miss. When I say that your future is guaranteed to be brighter than the past, I am not encouraging you to engage in wishful thinking. I am encouraging you to look to the solid truths of God's promises.

I know that the pain may feel raw and almost breathtaking, but I assure you that if you will dare look forward to the promises of God, the grip of pain and "had I knowns" will fade away, because God will come through for you. He is an expert in wiping away tears. He is the comforter, but He requires you to stop looking back. Do you remember Lot's wife? The angels tell Lot and his wife in Genesis 19:17, "Escape for thy life; look not behind thee, neither stay thou in all the plain; escape to the mountain, lest thou be consumed." However, we see that Lot's wife looked back in Genesis 19:26: "But his wife looked back from behind him, and she became a pillar of salt." I am so grateful for this dispensation of the grace of God. We do not see people turning into pillars of salt, but can you see how detrimental it can be to not look forward and run with the words of deliverance and promise God has given us?

Looking back is dangerous. It will keep you grounded, and it will keep you oblivious to the onset of the miracle happening right in front of you. If you stay stuck in the past, you will literally become reduced to a pillar of salt. You will be static and unproductive, you will not be creating value, and you will just be stuck. Praise God that in Christ we have the power to move on. The hold of the past can't keep you down. Make small steps first, and then bigger steps, but keep moving forward. You cannot do anything about the past, but you can do everything with today and tomorrow. Yesterday is gone, but today is alive and well before you. Tomorrow is gearing up for you as well.

Take a look at the following scripture and see the mindset of God towards yesterday, today, and tomorrow: "Therefore let no man glory in men, For all things are yours: Whether Paul, or Apollos, or Cephas, or the world, or life, or death, OR THINGS PRESENT, OR THINGS TO COME: all are yours" (1 Corinthians 3:21–22).

Do you see that? Yesterday does not feature at all. Today and tomorrow have been given to you. Your yesterday has no effect on your outcomes today and tomorrow. Yesterday does not determine today or tomorrow. You can still be who God said you will be. You can still do what God said you will do. You can still have what God said you will have. God is in your today *and* tomorrow, and He has given this to you to dominate and run with and receive all He has for you!

Now take a look at what the scriptures say about yesterday. See what Paul says in Philippians 3:13–14: "Brethren, I count not myself to have apprehended: but this one thing I do, forgetting those things which are behind, and reaching forth unto those things which are before, I press toward the mark for the prize of the high calling of God in Christ Jesus."

Today is packed with God's goodness. Look around you, take stock, focus, and embrace and celebrate the faithfulness of God today. A man of faith that inspires me a lot once said that "the reason why you have not lost it all is because of God." As such, there is something to focus your thoughts on in the now to be thankful for. Now think of the future He has promised. What are you hurting about? Lay it before Him. He is the one that gives double for the trouble we have been through.

> For your shame ye shall have double; and for confusion they shall rejoice in their portion:

therefore in their land they shall possess the double: everlasting joy shall be unto them. (Isaiah 61:7)

Behold, at that time I will undo all that afflict thee: and I will save her that halteth, and gather her that was driven out; and I will get them praise and fame in every land where they have been put to shame. (Zephaniah 3:19)

God can even restore lost time. Joel 2:25 states, "And I will restore to you the years that the locust hath eaten, the cankerworm, and the caterpillar, and the palmerworm, my great army which I sent among you."

Keep looking forward to all God has for you, and you'll see and approach life differently. You'll definitely see restoration more than you ever expected or imagined. Please make sure that you are focused on the tangible promise in a given word of God. This makes all the difference, because God is His word and He cannot lie (Hebrews 6:18).

10

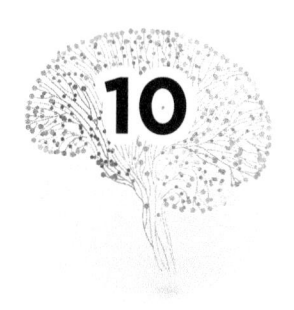

FREEDOM FROM INDECISION AND CONFUSION

Indecision can be a dangerous place to be; especially if you stay there perpetually and consistently. It births a state of confusion and lack of productivity. It will put your mind into chaos and will cause you to get depressed or stay depressed and not see any way out.

A state of indecision and confusion was the breaking point for me when I became severely depressed. As you may recall, I mentioned this in the details of my story in chapter 1. I kept going back and forth on a decision, and the chaos finally got the best of me.

"Do I do this, or do I do that?" "Should I stay here, or do I go there?" "Should I choose this, or should I choose that?" Do you find yourself constantly second-guessing your decisions? Do you make one and then change your mind and then change it again? I know too well how this can feel. People who are depressed often find it even more difficult than usual to make decisions. It is a very unstable state to be in. Praise God you do not have to remain like this and there is a way out!

The reason why indecision is an issue is because, as I said earlier, it breeds confusion. The scriptures are very clear about confusion. It is not from God. Anything not from God is entirely evil and should not be allowed to be present in our lives.

1 Corinthians 14:33 states, "For God is not the author of confusion, but of peace, as in all churches of the saints."

How, then, do you get out of this pit? Imagine you are in a well or a dark tunnel and you are trying to get out. You will need the steady, firm rungs of a ladder to hold on to and climb out of that well, or you will need a lamp to find a steady footing to walk out of the tunnel. Now, amidst the myriad thoughts and options being presented to you, and amidst the mix of life's experiences your decisions may be influenced by, there is a sure, steady path to which you can tie every decision you make, and you can never be wrong. I present to you the living Word of God. If you can link every decision you make to a firm word, you will always have a resting place for your soul, knowing that you have made the right decision and you are on the right path.

Making a Decision about Marriage

I remember when I and my partner got to the point in our relationship that I had to make that final commitment to taking the step of getting married. We had known each other for several years, and I knew I was going to get married to my now spouse. However, at the point of making the final decision to move forward, so many thoughts started coming to mind, this question and that question. Knowing I was going ahead with a decision I planned to never turn back on brought on some pressure. I had to sit with God and write down all the reasons why I wanted to go ahead with it. I put this beside the contrary thoughts that came, and then I put all these against God's Word. Based on God's Word, there was no reason why I should not go ahead. This was my light. I was able to walk on the Word and move forward and not stay stuck in indecision and confusion. God has been good; my marriage is blessed, and I am grateful.

David called the Word of God a lamp unto his feet and a lamp unto his path. You can say that for yourself. "Thy word is a lamp unto my feet, and a light unto my path." (Psalm 119:105). In practical terms, when you are not feeling certain and you ask the Holy Spirit to guide you, even if you feel as if you have not clearly heard a specific word concerning that situation, you can stand on the word that says the steps of a righteous person are ordered by God and then *take a step*, believing that the Holy Spirit is guiding you and that the Word applies to you. The most important thing you need to do is *believe God* to fulfil His end of the word and *order your steps!* You have got to come to a place where you believe God enough to know that because you are taking a step with prayer and knowledge, your steps will be ordered. This will free you from becoming frozen in the fear of making the wrong decision and allowing confusion to paralyze you.

The Purpose and the Plans of God

You see, God has "Godzillion" plans for your life. "Godzillion" is a term that I came up with to express what God spoke to me. You cannot outstep His plans. God showed me in a dream an image that describes this so clearly. I woke up in the morning on this day, and in my dream I saw two spheres: a large sphere and a smaller sphere underlying it. As I woke up with this image still in my mind's eye, I heard the Spirit of God speak to me.

Message

God's Purpose Underlies His Plans

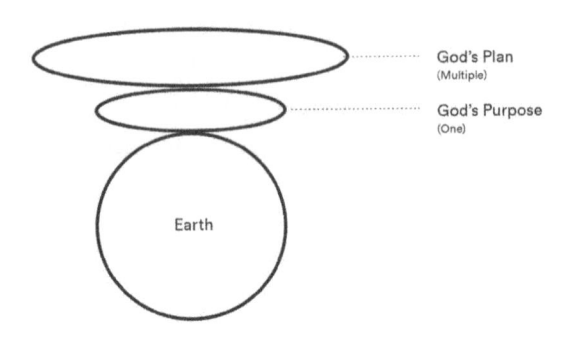

```
God's Plan (Multiple)
God's Purpose (One)
Earth
```

I woke up and heard Him say, "Nkiru, my purpose underlies my plans." God's plans are multiple. He has Godzillion unending ways of achieving what He wants. You cannot miss it when you are in Him, but He has one purpose with you and me, and that is to make us conformed to the image of Jesus, the firstborn of our awesome family! Do you get it? Multiple plans, one purpose! You won't miss it. Just focus on loving Abba.

Romans 8:28–29 states, "And we know that all things work together for good to them that love God, to them who are the called according to his purpose. For whom he did foreknow, he also did predestinate to be conformed to the image of his Son, that he might be the firstborn among many brethren." So you see, you can have peace, knowing that everywhere you go, God is leading you. You have got to believe this, and it will work for you. Remember, it is unto you according to your faith. Never remain confused. Scriptures say a double-minded person cannot receive anything from God. The Lord is your Shepherd (Psalm 23). The Lord is the Shepherd and Bishop of your soul (1 Peter 2:25). A shepherd is one who guides or directs in a particular direction. This means you have a guide. He won't lose you. He will leave the ninety-nine sheep to find His lost sheep in you. Do not be afraid of getting lost.

Walk with confidence. Make bold, decisive, Word-inspired, Holy Spirit–guided steps by fellowshipping with your Father and moving forward. You will see yourself come to a point where you will be out of that pit and out of that tunnel, and light will shine so brightly all around you. You won't hear horrible voices in your head any more. You will only have peace, because you will only be hearing the voice you should hear—the voice of the Shepherd. "My sheep hear my voice, and I know them, and they follow me" (John 10:27 KJV).

11

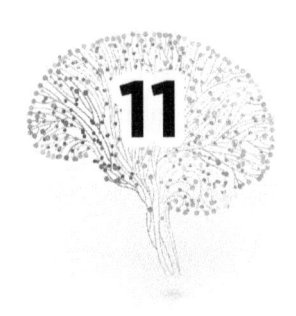

FREEDOM FROM HURTS

Some people have had terrible things done to them. They have been hurt by people who should have been there to protect and love them. Some people have also hurt themselves by doing things to themselves they do not think they can ever get beyond. All sorts of things have happened to people that seem irreversible or never to be redeemed. What if your spouse leaves you after twenty years of marriage? What if you have been raped? What if someone killed your loved one? What about abuse—sexual, physical, or verbal? The list can go on and on. What if you did something you cannot get over? Did you break the hearts of dear loved ones who looked up to you? The list can go on, can't it?

No matter how dark it becomes, nothing—and I mean absolutely nothing—is beyond the reach of God's love. Your pain is unique to you, and I am not even going to try to belittle it, but there is someone who knows exactly how you feel, and He decided to trade your pain with His joy. Jesus bore your pain, your grief, and your sorrow. There is nothing you are feeling now that He did not experience. He knew the pain of rejection, the pain of betrayal, the pain of false accusation, the pain of disgrace, and the pain of literally everything you can think of. He took it so you don't have to.

The scripture says He is a high priest who is familiar with our infirmities.

> For we do not have a High Priest who is unable to sympathize *and* understand our weaknesses *and* temptations, but One who has been tempted [knowing exactly how it feels to be human] in every respect as *we are, yet* without [committing any] sin. (Hebrews 4:15 AMP)
>
> Surely He has borne our grief and carried our sorrows; yet we esteemed Him stricken, smitten by God, and afflicted. But He *was* wounded for our transgressions, *He was* bruised for our iniquities; the chastisement for our peace *was* upon Him, and by His stripes we are healed. (Isaiah 53:4–6 NKJV)

Jesus tells us that the key to receiving the trade-off is to forgive. The key to freedom from hurts is forgiveness. You do not have to carry that responsibility of payback any more to give yourself the chance to live, the chance to breathe, and the chance to heal. Let it go. You perpetuate the harm done to you when you hold on to it. Many illnesses are linked to unforgiveness in your heart. God is hindered from doing all the good He wants to do in your life because unforgiveness is stifling His flow in you. It is like a rubber insulator inhibiting the flow of electricity. This is why, in Mark 11: 24–25, He shows you He is willing to give you anything you ask for but asks that you forgive if you have anything against anyone. "Therefore I say unto you, What things soever ye desire, when ye pray, believe that ye receive them, and ye shall have them. And when ye stand praying, forgive, if ye have ought against any: that your Father also which is in heaven may forgive you your trespasses" (Mark 11:24–25).

It may seem impossible to you, but let me share with you that you are not expected to do this on your own. All you have to do is ask Father God to help you. His grace is available where you are weak. Open up and tell Him you are struggling. Look into what He says. Ask for help and do what He says. Just take that step. The minute you take that step towards forgiveness—not waiting to feel like doing it, but just going ahead by faith—the release you will feel will be so beautiful. You will realize that it cost you more to hold on than to let go.

Tips for Forgiving Others

Here are some steps you can take to get to the point of letting go and forgiving:

- Recognize that you have been forgiven a debt that would have cost you your eternity. Oh wow, doesn't that just humble you? Even more impressive is the fact that you weren't asking for this. You were still going off on your own way, and God loved you still. You rejected Him, but He loved you still and died for you so that you can live for Him. And now He has given you access to Him forever, made you righteous, extended His unending grace, and called you His own, and you did not initiate any of this. The moment you can understand the love of God for you, you will be compelled by love, and no evil will be too dark to hold you in the bondage of unforgiveness.
- See beyond the physical person who hurt you. It is never really about the person. There is an enemy that tries so hard to cause strife amongst us by playing tricks on our minds. A person may have done what he or she did because the person did not know any better and fell for the many tricks the enemy plays in our minds with thoughts inspiring all the hurt done. You can also say that for yourself. Don't fight the

wrong person; fight the enemy. Fight with love—love for that person and love for yourself. Let go. "For we wrestle not against flesh and blood, but against principalities, against powers, against the rulers of the darkness of this world, against spiritual wickedness in high places" (Ephesians 6:12).

My Experience of Forgiving and Letting Go

I have learnt forgiveness on many levels, but I'll share one occasion where I learnt this first-hand when my Father passed on. While visiting family, a couple of men drew up behind his car, threatened him, and shot at him. My dad did not survive this. We were later told that these men were looking for someone else who looked like my dad. Whatever the case, he was no longer here with us. My thoughts after it happened were "Why? How can anyone kill? How can anyone choose to end another person's life?" And the answer was clear. That's the influence of the enemy on a yielded mind. I could not bring myself to go down the path of unforgiveness or hatred towards these people. If I ever meet them, I will ask them why they did it. I will be interested in knowing their thought processes leading towards their acts, but I will not allow my heart to be burdened with hatred. It would only cause me harm if I did. I thank God He has shown me a better way. I have come to understand who the real enemy is, and since this happened, in response, more than ever before, I decided instead to be more driven to destroy the works of the enemy and shine as a light in this dark world through God's love and power, in every way I can in my circle of influence. I decided to have the attitude that Jesus had after He heard His cousin John had been murdered in Matthew 14:13–14. He went away to be by Himself, and I totally get that. You will need that time and space to get yourself together. But almost immediately, He left that place and went and healed the sick and preached the gospel, destroying the works of darkness, moved by compassion. You see, we overcome evil with good. Forgive the person involved and fight the real enemy.

This is the point I would like you to understand. You step on the enemy's face when you respond to hurt with love.

A simpler example of a recent time when I learnt forgiveness by not operating in my capacity came following a conversation with my husband. I felt hurt by something he said, and I wanted to hold back and saw myself walking the path to holding a grudge. I knew I could not afford to do this, because walking out of love stifles the Spirit and goes against the commandment of love. I ran to my room, shut the door, told God how upset I was, spoke in tongues, and then relaxed. I heard Him say, "Forgive."

I said to Him, "I don't feel like it. How could he say this and that?"

And then I heard again "Forgive."

So I said, "OK, I'll read the scriptures a bit and get my heart fed with the Word, because I know it's my life source." As I meditated on scriptures, I came to Ephesians 4, and I was undone. I again saw God's love requirement of love and unity, and I just could not do otherwise. I took steps of faith and came around to making peace, and it was just beautiful. Peace, love, and laughter flowed. Honestly, the grudge would have cost me more energy. I really believe Jesus when He said, "My yoke is easy, and my burden is light." The yoke of the enemy is terrible. When you lose your life for Jesus's sake, you actually find it. In that moment, I found life by letting go of my desires; I found it all by God enabling me. He is willing and able to help you out of being stuck in unforgiveness.

- Finally, don't be misguided into thinking that God was responsible for the hurt you experienced. The enemy came to steal, to kill, and to destroy. He is the one trying to cause havoc. Praise God, Jesus came that we may have life to the full till it overflows. The Bible says every good and perfect gift comes from God the Father. If it is not good, it is not God. This is so important to know, because some people are angry with God for letting certain things go wrong, and in a sense they feel hurt by Him. This is an awful situation to be in. If you think that the God of all comfort is the one who caused you harm, where else can you then run? Can I just let you know that on the earth, God gave man dominion and authority over the affairs that govern the earth, and a lot of things happen not because He allows them to but because of the fall of humanity. Hold on. Do not get upset at this point. Just stay with me.

God is a good God. He has given us all things that pertain to life and godliness. He does not lie, and He does not fail. He stays true to His word. When something goes terribly wrong and we try to figure out why, it is almost tempting to lay responsibility on Him, but He is the constant and not the variable. When a plane crashes, we do not question the force of gravity; we begin to think about what could have gone wrong with the plane. Personally, I see that when something happens, that is not positive, I look back to reassess and see what the knowledge gap was from my end. God says in His Word that His people perish for lack of knowledge. Even if I do not find any clear reason, I choose to continue to see God as He says He is. God is good, and His mercies endure forever.

Unforgiveness hurts you more than you realize. For any evil that's been done to you, for any hurts you have experienced, forgive and be free.

> … forgive and you shall be forgiven. (Luke 6:37)

> And be ye kind one to another, tenderhearted, forgiving one another, even as God for Christ's sake hath forgiven you. (Ephesians 4:32)

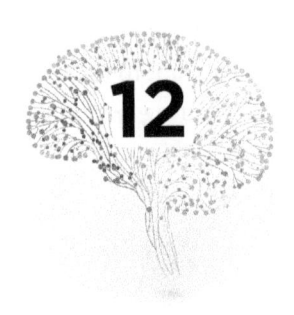

FREEDOM FROM GRIEF

I still remember when my husband told me that my dad did not make it. It all happened really quickly. We heard one evening that both of my parents had encountered some gunmen, and the next thing I knew, I was told he had been shot and hadn't made it. I am not going to stay fixed on the emotions that played out at this time, but I'll just say a bit. There were feelings of disbelief. I felt a huge aching in my heart, increased sensitivity to sounds and the environment, a feeling of unreality, and a huge sense of "How can this be?" But amidst it all, there was a great, great presence of the comfort and embrace of God's love.

The pain of the loss of a loved one can almost feel suffocating, but God is close to the broken-hearted. In those moments, His comfort is right there; you just have to embrace it. He knows the tears, and He knows the hurt. He understands. I do not mince any words when I say He understands. Your experience of grief may feel isolated to you, because no one can really say he or she shared the same attachments you shared with your loved one, but you've got to believe that Jesus has been where you have been. So when He gives you words of comfort by His Spirit in those moments, believe Him.

God's Comfort for You

A number of people reading this book may have experienced the loss of a loved one, and their experiences are unique to them. No one can undermine them, and I do not try to. One thing that I do know is true for all is that God is indeed close to the broken-hearted and understands. In those moments of grief, God will be speaking words of comfort to you, or He will send people your way with words to comfort you or just be there for you. Please do not push people away, and very importantly, do not push God away in anger. I'll explain in a bit. Now is the time to embrace His comfort and love as never before.

> Blessed be God, even the Father of our Lord Jesus Christ, the Father of mercies, and the God of all comfort: Who comforteth us in all our tribulation, that we may be able to comfort them which are in any trouble, by the comfort wherewith we ourselves are comforted of God. (2 Corinthians 1:3–4)

> Nevertheless God, that comforteth those that are cast down, comforted us by the coming of Titus. (2 Corinthians 7:6)

Watch out for comfort from God Himself both directly and from the people He sends to you; just as He sent Titus to Paul, and yield to this comfort. I remember when, shortly after my dad went to be with God, I was still grieving. I was walking down a street near my home, just thinking about my dad, and it was hurting so much in that moment. I was feeling down. Then I got into my car and was being driven home by a family friend. The radio was on, and the lady speaking on the radio then said she was about to play a song, and that song was the hymn "How Great Thou Art"! That was one of my dad's favourite songs! I was shocked, because it was not like it was a Sunday morning, when Christian music was usually played. One normally does not hear that kind of song on a secular radio station in the afternoon during the week! I knew God was comforting me. I sang along, and I knew in my heart during moments like that, that Dad was safe with God. My dear friend, look out for the comfort he is sending out to you. He is there with you.

My husband was also a major source of comfort to me. I kept hearing the word about how Isaac got comforted by Rebecca when his mum passed on. In that period, my husband did such sweet things and was such a huge source of comfort. I could see that scripture playing out. I could see that God was using him. Look around you. Are people coming to you who are trying to help you get out of grief? Do not push them away. Rather, allow yourself to be comforted. Do not isolate yourself.

Jesus Wept

Personally, when I look through the scriptures, I see some points when Jesus experienced the loss of a loved one. When outside the grave of Lazarus, He wept (John 11:35). Also, after His cousin John passed on, He went off to be alone (Matthew 14:13). Remember: He was a man, although he was also God. The reason I am emphasizing that He understands and that He was a man as well as God is because He models for us what we have the capacity to do, being men inhabited by God. He shows us we can overcome because He overcame. We can move forward. We will heal. Joy comes in the morning. We have an everlasting, living confident hope!

Hebrews 4:15 states, "For we have not an high priest which cannot be touched with the feeling of our infirmities: but was in all points tempted like as we are, yet without sin." Praise God! In all these things, we are more than conquerors through Christ, who loves us (Romans 8:37). If we follow His example, we can see He rose up from the feeling of grief. He did not allow Himself to wallow in it.

We can rise above grief. Remember: we do not sorrow as though we have no hope. We can set our eyes on the resurrection that is promised and continue to live victoriously with hope. I would like to say here that even here on earth, to those that believe, you can do what Jesus did and promised that we would be able to do right in the face of death. He promised us that we would raise the dead. Go for it! One way or another, we win in the end!

One thing is certain—the Holy Spirit is our comforter and He knows exactly what we need. Listen to Him, and let Him carry you through. God is the source of all comfort.

When I Think About My Dad

Having a new perspective of death has changed the way I think when I remember my dad. This perspective I have allowed me to heal quickly. When I think about Dad, I remember the good times, but as opposed to the finality that death presents, I have a forward-looking expectation that I've built really strongly. I know I am going to see him again, so I look forward to this a lot! It is going to be grand! You see, this is what Jesus has done for us! There is no mystery to death any more. Death has been defeated by Him.

A Different Perspective of Death

I find that one of the reasons why death seems such a huge blow is the perspective of death that has been entrenched in our minds apart from the pain of separation. I would like to encourage you by helping you change your perspective about death.

There are four important things to note regarding death:

1. Death is not final (1 Thessalonians 4:16). The dead in Christ will rise again. That sense of finality has been passed

on from the world, because they do not believe. It is only a matter of time before we all see our loved ones again.

2. We and our loved ones are safe in God's love (Romans 8:38–39). Even death cannot separate us from the love of God. This does not mean we should desire death in any way. Paul says in 2 Corinthians 5:4 (NLT) "While we live in these earthly bodies, we groan and sigh, but it's not that we want to die and get rid of these bodies that clothe us. Rather, we want to put on our new bodies so that these dying bodies will be swallowed up by life."

3. God is not to blame. Every good and perfect gift is from the Father (James 1:17). During my time of grief, I knew it was not God that did this. I knew God is good. I ran to Him and stayed in His loving embrace, which was more than I had ever experienced. At that time, I knew that even if I did not understand where things went wrong, I knew enough to know God is good and there is an enemy. As stated in 1 Corinthians 15:26, "The last enemy that shall be destroyed is death." Don't make God the enemy when all you need is His love.

4. Christ has destroyed the one with the power of death and delivered us from the fear of death.

"Forasmuch then as the children are partakers of flesh and blood, he also himself likewise took part of the same; that through death he might destroy him that had the power of death, that is, the devil; and deliver them who through fear of death were all their lifetime subject to bondage" (Hebrews 2:14–15). Death is done for! It is dealt with! It is a defeated foe! Laugh in its face! The sting is gone. Taunt death like Paul did in 1 Corinthians 15:55 and say, "Where oh death is your sting, where oh death is your victory?" Yes! Taunt death. Our king has defeated death! Praise God! Soon it will be utterly destroyed.

Refuse to wallow constantly in what-ifs. Refuse to let the spirit of heaviness rest on you permanently. I encourage you to cry in God's arms, because indeed, there is a time to cry and a time to laugh. But don't keep crying for too long. Laugh with a laughter of joy, knowing that God loves you and God is on your side. Laugh knowing that it will be clear one day what happened. Never move an inch from trusting God because of your experience. Laugh, knowing that the resurrection day is coming.

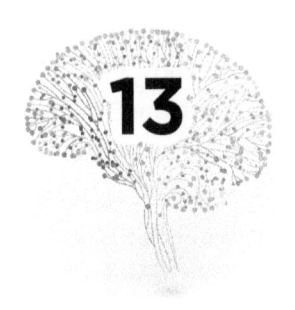

LIVING WITH JOY: ABIDING IN LOVE

Joy is so vital because it produces strength. Have you ever felt so tired physically, and all of a sudden you heard good news and became energized almost immediately? This happens because strength, vitality, and vigour are directly linked to how joyful you are. To go through life, therefore, you can see that it is key for us to remain joyful. We just cannot afford to live without joy. The joy of the Lord is our strength. "Then he said unto them, Go your way, eat the fat, and drink the sweet, and send portions unto them for whom nothing is prepared: for this day is holy unto our Lord: neither be ye sorry; for the joy of the Lord is your strength" (Nehemiah 8:10)

Some people go to sleep and wake up unrefreshed because their minds never go to sleep. This is often the case in depressed people; they are likely to always be tired and have no drive.

Beginning to live every moment with an awakened consciousness to God's love will change this. This is what it means to abide in His love.

Abiding in God's love means being awakened to God's love for you and pouring this love out to others. This opens up the fountain of joy within. As a believer, there is joy in your spirit. This is one dimension of the fruit of the Spirit. Living conscious of God's love and sharing it with others will open up this fountain for you.

In the book of John, Jesus talks about abiding in God's love and loving others as a sure source of maintaining His joy to the full in our lives.

John 15: 9–13 states, "As the Father hath loved me, so have I loved you: continue ye in my love. *If ye keep my commandments, ye shall abide in my love*; even as I have kept my Father's commandments, and abide in his love. *These things have I spoken unto you, that my joy might remain in you, and that your joy might be full.* This is my commandment, that ye love one another, as I have loved you. Greater love hath no man than this; that a man lay down his life for his friends" (emphasis added).

From the verses above, you can see that Jesus shows us how we can have His joy remain in us and be full. Essentially, to have His joy remain in us and be full, we just have to abide in His love and obey His commandment, which is to love others.

Jesus Loves Nkiru; How I Abide in Love

The heading looks interesting, doesn't it? Ha! Of course Jesus loves you too. The reason I used this as the heading was to drive home a point that helps me a lot with abiding in God's love.

I *personalize the love of God,* and I do this *audibly* and *visibly.*

Sometimes we get caught up with the truth that God so loved the "world" that we forget He actually meant you and me where the word "world" was used. I find that when I take the time to think about this reality, say it to myself audibly, talk about it, and relish it in my heart, it becomes more and more ingrained in me.

There have been periods when I haven't felt the love of God, but in those moments, I have remembered 1 John 4:16: "And we have *known* and *believed* the love that God hath to us. God is love; and he that dwelleth in love dwelleth in God, and God in him" (emphasis added).

I would remind myself that firstly I "know" God loves me and that secondly I "believe" He loves me. Feelings come secondary. I then go on to say to myself, "now that I know this and believe this, how do I respond to this?" I then take active steps based on this truth. This gives me a stability and a foundation for joy that cannot be taken away.

The beautiful thing is that God still shows up and confirms His word, making me even "feel" loved from time to time.

When I get refuelled this way, I am able to release this love to others and my joy is full.

More on Abiding in God's Love

To abide in His love is to live conscious of His love and to be awakened to His love. It means having the realization that God loves you rather than just recognizing "God loves you" as a common phrase people use. Living conscious of this reality resulting from a personal realization that He actually thinks about you, is fond of you, cares about you, and wants the best for you is a great joy bringer. Going ahead to spread this love ensures the constant flow of this joy.

Because He loves you, *you can rise* from the pitfalls of a poor self-image, knowing that you are worth the precious blood of Jesus and that you are loved by, valued by, wanted by, relevant to, special to, and seen as gifted by your heavenly Father. You can rise from the pit of fear, anxiety, and worry, knowing that no matter what has happened or is happening, your Father loves you, so you can cast your cares upon Him and be at peace.

You can rise from failure knowing that you have a destiny in Christ that is sure and that all things work together for your good because you love God and are called according to His purpose. You have no need to wallow in shame or defeat. You can stand on God's promise that for your shame He will give you double. You can rise from disappointment knowing that the path of the just shines brighter and brighter unto the perfect day (Proverbs 4:18); your future is bright, and it will outshine your present disappointment. You can rise from guilt because you know that when He looks at you, He does not see what you did wrong. Rather, He sees His Son in you, spotless and blameless because of His free gift of right standing in His sight.

You can rise from regret knowing that God is able to restore what you think has been lost, and He is willing to do so because He loves you. You can rise from indecision and confusion because He is your Shepherd and He will never leave you alone. You can rise from hurts knowing that because He loves you, He will make all things right in due time. He knows your pain and has felt your hurt. He is close to the broken-hearted, and He will not only make you whole but will also restore what was lost. You can rise from grief knowing that He is a comforter like no other and that His word is sure that joy comes in the morning.

Keep receiving His love daily. Wake up every morning thinking to yourself about how much you are loved and thought of fondly by your Daddy. Receive His love and let it fill up your vessel to overflowing so you can go out and pour this love out to others. Keep receiving, because He never stops giving. Our Father is love Himself. Wake up to His love. Be sure of His love and never doubt it. Let it keep you steady. Be rooted and grounded in His unconditional love and you'll become stable and whole like a tree planted by the streams of water that always bears its fruit in season. Your leaves will be evergreen. Your days will be like heaven on earth. When challenges come, you will not be overcome, but you will overcome them because you are full of your Daddy.

Ephesians 3:17–19 (paraphrased) states, "Being rooted and grounded in love that you may be filled with all the fullness of God."

Loving Others

It is truly difficult to remain depressed when you get your mind off yourself and intentionally and actively seek to bless others. A depressed person usually has his or her mind solely focused on himself or herself. When depressed, you find yourself thinking about your imperfections, hurts, misfortunes, pain, or guilt. The focus is usually on self. There is time for everything. There may be a time of initial pain that causes you to be absorbed in yourself, but there has to be a time when you decide to look into the future with hope and anticipation by faith. At this point, it is so key to get your mind off you. Look around you and think of ways to make someone else smile. You may not feel like doing so, but do not wait to feel any emotion. Just go ahead and act on God's Word here by loving people, and you will see your emotions of joy restored.

I remember intentionally going out of my comfort zone to engage in conversations with friends—not to talk about my circumstances but to allow myself to be an ear to them. This is very beneficial to you, because isolation aggravates depression. Get out of being alone. Attend gatherings, offer your help, and give your mind the job of thinking constructively about another person. Look for ways to meet the needs of people around you, and trust God to take care of you. You will begin to notice the heaviness lifting, and it will be so refreshing to your soul.

What does it look like to love other people? It is clear what love looks like in 1 Corinthians 13. Love is patient, love is kind, it does not envy, it does not boast, it is not proud, it is not rude, it is not self-seeking, it is not easily angered, it keeps no record of wrongs, it does not delight in evil, it rejoices with the truth, it always protects, it always trusts, it always hopes, it always perseveres, and it never fails.

Love is a choice. Love will birth feelings, but love itself is not a feeling. Love decides to give itself unconditionally. Love should drive you. This is what you are made of. This God kind of love has been truly shed abroad in your heart by the Holy Spirit. I always say, "We were made by Love Himself to be loved and to love. You can never go wrong with love. There is no law against love. Love never fails. A life of joy is full of love."

14

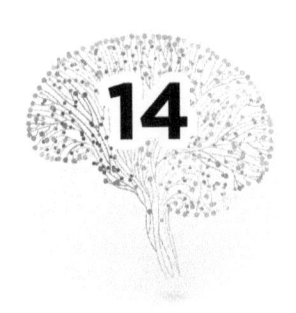

LIVING WITH JOY: KNOWING YOUR IDENTITY

Realizing who you are as a son or daughter of God will change your outlook on any situation you are in right now. Try in this moment to think of the term "son" or "daughter" as the word is used in our day-to-day human lives, without a religious connotation. Yes, yes! That is it! Actual sons and daughters of God—that is who we are. This means so many things, and underlying all this is fundamentally a relationship. God loves you and me, His kids. As His child, you have a place in His house.

Personally, when I realized that I was a daughter of God, a lot of things shifted for me. This realization revolutionized my thought processes. I began to cast my cares on God, and I stopped being fretful and anxious. I saw myself drastically change for the better. I was no longer trying to measure up to any standards, and I was not trying to be perfect any more. I was no longer uncertain of my value and judging my worth based on people's words or my achievements, which was like living on a roller coaster because of the variations this brought about. I became assured of my value in God. I knew I was worth the blood of Jesus. I knew I had been accepted and perfect in Christ, and that only God's word about me, not man's words, is authority. As for my achievements or accomplishments, my focus is giving the Father God glory and fulfilling my call. They are no longer a determination of my value.

Knowing who you are helps you identify when the enemy is lying to you with all sorts of contrary suggestions. It is only when you know the truth that you can identify and resist the lie. As a born-again child of God, your spirit is created anew—perfect in God's eyes, with His nature and His wisdom. In fact, 2 Timothy 1:7 says, "For God hath not given us the spirit of fear, but of power, love and a sound mind." This is the real you. The real you is a spitting image of Jesus. When you accept that this is who you are, then you realize that fear is foreign. It is not you, so you can rise boldly over it by being assured of your Father's love. This is why scripture admonishes us to not be conformed to the world but to be transformed by the renewal of our minds. Your spirit is perfect, but your mind needs to be renewed daily with the Word of Truth, and your flesh and your physical experience will follow.

Remember: you are not what you feel. You are what you think, and what you think is a product of what you believe. Behold God's Word as regards your identity, and the Word of Truth will sanctify you and cleanse you, removing all the lying impurities the Devil tried to stick on you. You will begin to see you for who you are. You will see that you were born by Love Himself, to be loved and to love. You will see you were born for a purpose, with value, and that you are wanted, cherished, beloved, endowed, and gifted by a God who is indeed your Father and longs for you to showcase His glory and enjoy Him.

When I say, "Behold the Word," I mean dive into the Word, soak it in, and give the Word of God all your attention, with your eyes and with your ears. Let it fill your heart. It will work in you to transform you by the power of the Spirit of God.

Know Who You Are

Knowing who you are is so important. Everything you say and do—your dreams, your aspirations, the way you carry yourself, and the perception you have of yourself—is all tied to who you believe you are. *Who are you?* What informs the response you have given to that question? Is it what people say about you? Is it your past? Could it be your mistakes? Is it your environment? Where have you drawn that information from? Where do you get your narrative of who you are? Now let's shatter every wrong negative thought about you and replace it with *truth*.

You are God's child. You have His nature. You are just like Him. You have got to believe this and let it change the way you think about yourself. This is what it means to renew your mind. Let His narrative of you change your narrative of yourself. You have not been given a spirit of fear but a spirit of power, a spirit of love, and a sound mind. So you are powerful and loving, and you have an excellent mind. Live this way. To live less is to deny yourself. Teach your mind or train your mind to know who you really are. Do not let the world confuse you. You are the child of a king. You are royalty. You have a heart of compassion. You are the light of the world. When you step in, things become better for everyone. You are carrying answers for a generation. You are a blessing. You are gifted. You make good things happen. You live intentionally. You are valuable, and you are important in the scheme of life. You are relevant and you are needed; the world needs your light, and the world needs your salt. You have purpose, you have been called, you have been selected, you have been chosen, you have been ordained, and you are here now in life, making your own debut. You were born for such a time as this. Generations have come and gone, but now you are on stage. Your circle of influence needs you to be the best God has made you. The world is waiting for you daily to be all you are to be, for creation awaits the manifestation of the sons of God. You are an heir of the world! (Romans 4:13). God is your Daddy. The world is truly your oyster. Think this way and live this way!

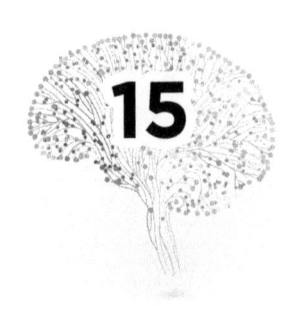

LIVING WITH JOY: THE POWER OF PRAISE AND THANKSGIVING

It is difficult to be truly thankful and depressed at the same time. There must be a give somewhere when you are truly thankful. If you and I decide to change our perspectives towards whatever seems to be weighing us down, and if we just let ourselves think along the lines of the good things happening in our lives, we will suddenly begin to have hope well up inside us. We'll start seeing that God has actually been good. Our brains will start releasing signals for happy hormones. We will begin to feel lighter. Thanksgiving instantly changes one's mood. If you remain thankful consistently and make this a lifestyle, it will be tremendously difficult for the enemy to pin you down again with thoughts that harbour depression.

Look around in the past and in the present. Actively seek what you should be thankful for. Look into the future through God's Word and intentionally start counting your blessings, and verbalize your thanks to Him. This is a weapon of war. Praising God and thanking God will cause His presence to envelop you and make the darkness flee. This is because God inhabits the praise of His people.

But thou *art* holy, *O thou* that inhabitest the praises of Israel. (Psalm 22:3)

To appoint unto them that mourn in Zion, to give unto them beauty for ashes, the oil of joy for mourning, the garment of praise for the spirit of heaviness; that they might be called trees of righteousness, the planting of the LORD, that he might be glorified. (Isaiah 61:3)

An Experience of Overcoming with Praise and Thanksgiving

I was at work one day, and it was one of those days that seem to bring a lot of pressure. I began to feel weary. I also began to think about how much I had to do in such little time. I work as a GP in the UK, and there are days that can be full of pressure. I noted that my countenance began to be downcast. I immediately recognized this and determined not to allow it to settle. Remember: the fruit of the Spirit is joy, and joy is your strength. In my past life, I would have taken this as just one of those moments and wallowed in it, but no more. I started writing about how thankful I was for my job. I thanked God for providing it for me, and I remembered when my husband and I prayed for it and the exams I passed on the way towards getting this job. I thanked God for the fact I was a practising medical doctor, and I remembered when I was told I might not be able to become one. I went back into time and started thanking God for a car accident I had been involved in, in which I sat on the side of the vehicle that was not hit by the oncoming truck and my life was spared. I thanked God for my son, who is now in excellent health, who did not breathe properly at birth. I thanked God for my husband, who is such a blessing to me, for all God was doing in his life. I went on and on, and by the time I was done, I was crying tears of joy. I was so blessed and lifted that the gloom or heaviness that tried to settle was totally annihilated. Ha, ha, ha! I was full of joy. I felt as if I had used a fully loaded machine gun and got rid of the little devil that had tried to come for my peace. This is how I live with joy.

The weapons of our warfare are not carnal, but they are mighty, through God, in the pulling down of strongholds. We take thoughts captive and bring them into subjection to the Word of God (2 Corinthians 10:4–5). We do this daily. We must always remember it is a battle that is fought in the mind. The beautiful thing is that it is easier to choose joy than to give in to negative toxic thoughts. Negative toxic thoughts may appear to be more appealing, but they will take up your energy and leave you drained and out of faith. Choose joy from the get-go and you'll be lifted, walking in peace, and whole.

Preserve Our Joy

Preserving our joy and holding our peace is a battle, but it is a good one because it is won for us already. All we have to do is just stand in the liberty that we have been granted by choosing well. The Bible says we are to labour to enter rest (Hebrews 4:11). It almost sounds like an oxymoron, doesn't it? Jesus paid for your peace. Jesus paid for your rest. Jesus paid for you to have a stress-free, peaceful, and enjoyable life, but it always comes down to a choice. Jesus is saying we must choose to be thankful. Don't complain, don't moan, don't be moody, and don't be gloomy. It is better to be grateful. Choose life.

Following are some scriptures that show how vital it is to be thankful.

"In everything give thanks: for this is the will of God in Christ Jesus concerning you" 1 Thessalonians 5:18. This means there is always something to be thankful for.

"As ye have therefore received Christ Jesus the Lord, so walk ye in him: Rooted and built up in him, and stablished in the faith, as ye have been taught, abounding therein with thanksgiving" (Colossians 2:6–7). Wow! Do you see here that we should abound with thanksgiving? I looked up the meaning of the word "abound" to find synonyms. I like to look at synonyms to help me appreciate words even better, and these are the synonyms I found for the word "abound": "To be full of", "to overflow with", "to teem with", "to be packed with", "to be crowded with", "to be thronged with", and "to be jammed with".

This is how thankful we should be always.

"By him therefore let us offer the *sacrifice of praise* to God *continually*, that is, *the fruit of our lips giving thanks to his name*" (Hebrews 13:15, emphasis added) If you can learn to be thankful and practise this consistently, you will find a sure and steadfast way of always being full of joy, and you will find that the enemy will truly find it difficult holding you down with the weight of depression. Praise is a weapon! Praising God creates an atmosphere full of His presence. The Bible says that God inhabits the praises of His people.

"But thou art Holy, o thou that inhabitest the praises of Israel" (Psalm 22:3). The spirit of depression cannot stand the atmosphere of praise. When you sing God's praises, that heaviness lifts. If you continue in praises, the spirit of depression will be exiled from your presence.

Do you remember when Saul was depressed and only the music played by David was able to give him any succour (1 Samuel 16:23)? You do not need to understand how this works, but if you will, in that moment of heaviness, open your mouth and sing—and I mean sing aloud and continue singing—you'll be delighted to see how light you'll begin to feel. Get a music player, put earphones in your ear, and get some good playlists with lots of joyful praises to your Father. Sing and dance in your Father's presence. Thank Him for all He has done, and watch amazing things happen.

The Effect of Music on the Brain

Research shows that music has significant positive effects on mood and the brain. A 2006 Harvard study of sixty adults with chronic pain found that music was able to reduce pain, depression, and disability. It is a no-brainer that this is the case. Our Father God has created it this way. This is why we are encouraged to sing praises throughout the scriptures.

Let me share another moment in scripture where the power of praise is displayed. This time it was with King Jehoshaphat (2 Chronicles 20). His army physically looked outnumbered, but after he and his people sought the Lord, the battle strategy was for the singers to go in front and sing praises to God. They sang, "Our God is good and His mercies endureth forever! Our God is good and His mercies endureth forever!" And the enemy camps basically attacked themselves! I thoroughly enjoy this story. In fact, I have my own personal song I have created based on this victorious song, which I sing during moments when I want to see the glorious presence of my Father in the affairs of my life. I really believe that when I sing this song, angels hear it as a battle cry and go forth to do God's word over my life.

Everyone going through depression needs to sing songs of praise! Remember that every good and perfect gift comes from the Father. Is there anything good in your life? Thank Him for it. He is the reason it is there. Wear the garment of praise. You have been given the garment of praise for the spirit of heaviness. Thank God, and sing His praises.

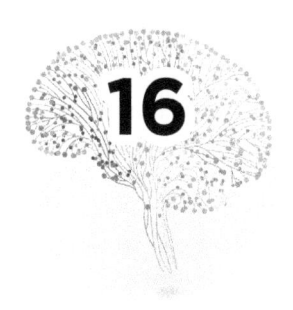

LIVING WITH JOY: THE POWER OF THOUGHTS

If you have never realized that your thoughts are powerful, please realize it today. I cannot overemphasize the importance of what you think as it relates to your feelings and your eventual reality. How you feel is a direct reflection of what you are thinking. If you want to feel different, you need to change what you are thinking. Sounds simple, right? A number of people I have met feel they are powerless over their feelings. The truth is that we can control the way we feel. It may not appear so at the start, but when you begin to take charge of your thoughts and remain persistent, you will see positive results.

I remember that back then I would just let my mind go wherever it wanted. I hadn't realized that we had a part to play in being responsible for what we allow our minds to focus on. Even if you take a medical prescription for depression, if you have not learnt to change the way you think and get rid of toxic thought patterns, you will likely fall into the same pit of depression again and again. Your thoughts are real substance. According to Christian neuroscientist Dr Caroline Leaf, our brains respond to our thoughts. When we think thoughts and make choices, these thoughts become real neural networks in the brain. The thought networks in the brain cause the release of signals that cause changes in our genes and DNA. This is called neuroplasticity. You can see that we literally are what we think. The things we think of most will grow. As Christians, this is not new to us. The scriptures say that as a man thinks in his heart, so is he (Proverbs 23:7).

If you are going to live with joy, you have to think thoughts that inspire joy. You will have to learn to be intentional about your thinking. You are not a victim of your thoughts. *You can choose.* I know it may feel as if negative thoughts just keep flooding in and you can't seem to control it. Don't worry; that is the enemy coming at you. He fights through thoughts, but you don't have to respond to those thoughts. Just keep focusing on what God says about His love for you, or His promises about whatever it is you are hopeful for. Respond to the thoughts inspired by God's Word with your words and actions. As you do this, the thoughts of the enemy, the negative thoughts that have been causing you so much distress, will gradually lose their hold on you. Remember: when we resist the enemy, he eventually flees (James 4:7). Your role is to keep your mind on the Father. He is the one who will give you peace.

Isaiah 26:3 states, "Thou wilt keep him in perfect peace, whose mind is stayed on thee: because he trusteth in thee." You can choose to focus on God and on His love and promises. I know it may look as though there is no future ahead, or it may seem as if what you are going through will never end, but choose to see a picture in your mind that shows you the future God wants for you with scriptures like Jeremiah 29:11 (KJV): "For I know the plans I have for you," declares the Lord, "plans to prosper you and not to harm you, to give you hope and a future."

How can you screen your thoughts to make sure you are thinking life-giving thoughts? Philippians 4:8 makes this very easy and clear to navigate: "Finally, brethren, whatsoever things are true, whatsoever things are honest, whatsoever things are just, whatsoever things are pure, whatsoever things are lovely, whatsoever things are of good report: if there be any virtue, and if there be any praise, think on these things."

If, for example, we consider looking at thoughts that are true, ask yourself, "Is what I am thinking about true?" If it does not line up with God's Word, it is not true. So if you are hearing in your mind that you are a failure, that you will never amount to anything, that you will fail, or any other kind of negative thought, you can emphatically know that all these are not true, because once you received Jesus and became God's child, you immediately became born again in your spirit and were blessed with every blessing of God and were given God's nature. This means that you are not a failure. You are destined to succeed, and your value is intrinsically defined by God's love for you, which can never, ever end. Isn't that just awesome? So this is how we can succeed at not falling for the pranks of the enemy. We take captive our thoughts and bring them into subjection to God's Word. Even if you are not depressed, this is something you must do daily.

"Casting down imaginations, and every high thing that exalteth itself against the knowledge of God, and bringing into captivity every thought to the obedience of Christ" (2 Corinthians 10:5). I just want to assure you right now that as God's child, you can hear Him. You know His voice. He is with you, and He is speaking to your spirit, telling you what you should know at this time. He is always speaking. Regardless of the negative thoughts, your Father's voice is speaking. Listen to Him. Remember that you will not follow the voice of a stranger, because the sheep knows the Shepherd's voice (John 10:3, 5). Even if it is so bad that you are hearing thoughts so loud that are now voices, your Father's voice is still speaking, and it will silence those negative voices. You were bought with a price, and you are God's property.

I declare in the name of Jesus that if you are hearing voices or seeing illusions, those voices and illusions are silenced now! Those illusions will cease to appear. I declare you have a sound mind in the name of Jesus! You will no longer hear voices that speak evil. You will hear only the voice of your Father that speaks comfort.

> My sheep hear my voice, and I know them, and they follow me. (John 10:27)

> And a stranger will they not follow, but will flee from him: for they know not the voice of strangers. (John 10:5)

Prayer

Father, thank you for clarity of thoughts for my readers. Thank you for sanctified thoughts. Thank you for wholesome thoughts, and thank you for life-giving thoughts.

17

LIVING WITH JOY: THE POWER OF WORDS

Words are powerful. They have creative ability. Words energize and words tear down. The power of life and death is released in words. Words are the creative force behind the universe. Words have effects that transcend from the spiritual realm to the physical realm, with effects that can be seen and felt in both realms. Words gave birth to us as children of God. God's Word is alive. I can show you scriptures to validate all I have just said about words, and I will, because we need to always remind ourselves.

Words are powerful:

> Death and life are in the power of the tongue: and they that love it shall eat the fruit thereof. (Proverbs 18:21 KJV)

Words have creative ability, and creation responds to words:

> And God said, Let there be light: and there was light. (Genesis 1:3 KJV)

And Jesus answered and said unto it, No man eat fruit of thee hereafter for ever. And his disciples heard it. (Mark 11:14)(KJV)

And in the morning, as they passed by, they saw the fig tree dried up from the roots. (Mark 11:20)(KJV)

It has been scientifically proven and documented that physical things respond to words. I tried this out twice in my home. I spoke to two halves of an apple that I divided and kept in similar conditions for a couple of days. To one half I spoke positive words, and to the other half I spoke negative words. The part which received positive words remained preserved, and the other part became rotten very quickly.

I did this again months later with two cups of rice, and I had the same results!

I like to give the example of Alexa, the Amazon product that responds to the spoken word, to show that even if we do not see the power released from our spoken words physically, words do release power which can be harnessed with physical effects.

Dr Emoto's Experiment

Dr Emoto was a scientist who discovered the effect of positive thoughts and words on water. He identified that water exposed to these positive thoughts and words formed beautiful crystals, but when negative thoughts and words were directed towards water, they formed distorted, randomly formed structures. When you think about the fact that humans are made up of 70 per cent water, that should get you thinking. You can then begin to imagine the impact our words have on us.

Words energize and words tear down:

> Like cold water to a weary soul is good news from
> a distant land. (Proverbs 25:25 KJV)

> The words of the reckless pierce like swords, but the tongue of the wise brings healing. (Proverbs 12:18 NIV)

> A merry heart doeth good like a medicine: but a broken spirit drieth the bones. (Proverbs 17:22 KJV)

Do you know that I can make you instantly begin to feel better by telling you good things about you or by talking about something good that has happened? You will feel a sense of well-being in your soul if I do so. In the same way, if I told you some bad news, you would immediately feel down inside.

The power of life and death is released in words.

> Death and life are in the power of the tongue: and they that love it shall eat the fruit thereof. (Proverbs 18:21 KJV)

> "The words of the reckless pierce like swords, but the tongue of the wise brings healing. (Proverbs 12:18 NIV)

The effect of words goes from the spiritual to the physical realm: "For the word of God is quick, and powerful, and sharper than any two-edged sword, piercing even to the dividing asunder of soul and spirit, and of the joints and marrow, and is a discerner of the thoughts and intents of the heart" (Hebrews 4:12 KJV).

Notice that the Word of God has an effect in the spirit, the soul, and then the physical body, based on this scripture. This sets the principle for how powerful words are. Praise God we can see that God's Word is most powerful; hence it is described as being sharper than any two-edged sword. Do you know why the Word of God is described as a sword? Remember that words are weapons. They can be used for good or bad. Do you remember that in Ephesians 6, the spoken Word of God is called the sword of the Spirit? Here is another scripture that shows you that words are weapons: "And he hath made my mouth like a sharp sword; in the shadow of his hand hath he hid me, and made me a polished shaft; in his quiver hath he hid me" (Isaiah 49:2 KJV).

The Word gave birth to us. "He chose to give us birth through the word of truth, that we might be a kind of firstfruits of all he created" (James 1:18 NIV).

We believed the word concerning Jesus dying for our sins and being resurrected; we spoke it out with our mouths and we became saved. "If you declare with your mouth, 'Jesus is Lord,' and believe in your heart that God raised him from the dead, you will be saved" (Romans 10:9).

Why Are Words So Important in Overcoming Depression?

I have taken a lot of time to show you above how important words are, because they are so key to you getting out of depression and living with joy. When you speak, things happen inside of you and all around you that you may not immediately see, but I tell you, things are happening. How do you want to feel? What do you want to see in your life? What challenge are you facing? All you have to do is get into the scriptures, find verses that are directly linked to what you are facing, and start speaking them out loud in the affirmative. What do I mean?

David says in Psalm 43:5 (KJV), "Why art thou cast down, o my soul? And why are thou disquieted within me? Hope in God: for I shall yet praise him, who is the health of my countenance, and my God." The Message translation puts it this way: "Why are you down in the dumps, dear soul? Why are you crying the blues? Fix my eyes on God—soon I'll be praising again, He puts a smile on my face. He's my God."

The key emphasis here is on self-talk! You've got to talk yourself back into victory with the Word of God.

Joshua 1:8 (KJV) states, "This book of the law shall not depart out of thy *mouth*; but thou shalt *meditate* therein day and night, that thou mayest observe to do according to all that is written therein: for then thou shalt make thy way prosperous, and then thou shalt have good success" (emphasis added). Notice it says not to let the word leave your *mouth*. In the original writings, the word "meditate" there meant "to mutter". Dear reader, write out things you want to see happening around you, and start saying they *are* happening! Tell yourself God's promises. Stick them all around you. Put them on your wall, in your screen savers, on your phone, and so on. Say them day and night. Don't say what you feel; *say what you want to feel!*

For example, here are some declarations you can say out loud now:

- My future is bright and glorious because the plans God has for me are plans of good and not evil, to give me a future and an expected end!
- I am born of God, I am God's child, and God loves me. He will never leave me or forsake me!
- I have the spirit of joy, so I am full of joy right now!
- I can do all things through Christ, who strengthens me!
- I enjoy good sleep because the Lord gives His beloved good sleep!
- My tomorrow is beautiful because God says so!
- Good things are happening to me because goodness and mercies are following me all the days of my life!
- I am excited about my days because God is for me!

- I am blessed! I will see the goodness of God in the land of the living!
- I have the spirit of power, the spirit of love, and a sound mind; as such, my mind is perfect.
- Forgetting the past, I press on to the mark of the high calling of God in Christ. I therefore let the past go and press on into my grand future.
- I have no fear!

Recently there was a moment when I had a sense of heaviness come on me for some reason. I had certain thoughts that were trying to weigh me down. Now, unlike before, I've learnt to be quick to not let this settle. I started thinking about the thoughts. By this I mean that I became conscious about what I was thinking. I screened my thoughts with Philippians 4:8, and I initially tried to just think myself away from them, but when I realized they weren't budging, I started speaking God's Word, and those thoughts faded. Don't forget that the enemy fights us with thoughts. The best way to overcome negative thoughts when they seem really strong is to start *speaking*. This is one of the longest chapters of this book because if you can harness your words, you can begin to change your environment and cause joy to spring up from inside you.

18

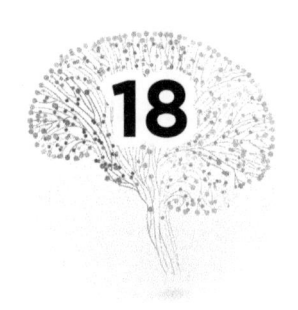

LIVING WITH JOY: THE POWER OF VISION

A person who is depressed has stopped looking ahead. Without vision, and without an image for tomorrow, you'll lose drive and you'll lose energy. "Where there is no vision, the people perish: but he that keepeth the law, happy is he" (Proverbs 29:18 KJV).

God always wants us looking forward. A lot of people feel tired all the time, and when they come to see doctors like me in the clinic, we cannot find any medical reason why. A lot of the time, it is because there is no drive for the future. These people are not living with a sense of purpose. There are no goals they are working towards. There is no image or vision for the future motivating them to move forward, and they might not realize it.

Leading up to when I became very depressed, my mind was stuck in the past, and when I was in the present, I was barely going through the motions and just moving with the flow of things. When I thought of the future, it was foggy, bleak, and negative. When God healed my mind, I started seeing myself in the future through the eyes of purpose, value, creativity, solution provision, and love. I started waking up with energy and excitement for my day, knowing I was a channel for God's love and power. God started showing me the future for my life as He had predestined, and this set me on a course for living with joy.

We were made to always have something to look forward to—to always be creating something new and learning something new. All over scripture, one can see the urge to keep moving forward. God told Moses to speak to the Israelites in Exodus 14:15 (KJV): "And the LORD said unto Moses, Wherefore criest thou unto me? Speak unto the children of Israel, that *they go forward*" (emphasis added).

We always have to be looking up and moving forward. To do this, we must consistently have an image in our minds that pulls us forward. This is what having a vision does. A vision activates within you the energy required for it. When you are depressed, you have stopped making mental images of the type of future that calls you forward. The pictures that are being created are usually pictures that release no life. They have no hope in them. These images are not from God. You will have to create images from His word to live with joy. Why am I speaking a lot about images? I am speaking a lot about images because we think in pictures. If I say "dog", a picture of a dog comes to your mind. You don't think the word "d-o-g". If I told you to help me get a glass of milk from your fridge, you would mentally picture yourself doing that and then go ahead and do it.

Your mind works with pictures, and this is the reason that if you think of your future and you see only images that speak of death and no hope, your entire being will respond by switching off like a computer system whose shutdown button has been pressed, and that hopelessness will become physical in you. If you see pictures of yourself victorious, winning, successful, healed, and loved, the life from that vision will be communicated to your entire being.

I remember the Holy Spirit telling me to place pictures on my wall. I put up pictures of family members, pictures of good times, and pictures of the future I would like to have, and I repeatedly looked at them and the Word of God supporting them. I was invariably giving my mind images that emitted life to me. In my current life, I still put images on my wall, along with scriptures, dreams, and possibilities I want to see in my life, as well as prophetic words. All these things help me see myself the way God has spoken over me, and it is working! Praise God, I am not using this method to come out of a pit, but I am using it to birth dreams and the vision God has placed in my heart. People call it having a vision board, but whatever you call it, please do it. The Bible speaks about making the vision clear and easy to read. Get a vision board for your life. Paste on it the images and pictures of your life that you want to see.

Habakkuk 2:2–3 states, "And the Lord answered me, and said, Write the vision, and make it plain upon tables, that he may run that readeth it." Your life can *never* go beyond what you have conceived in your mind. This is the reason that when God wanted to bless Abraham, He had to take him outside and show him the stars. He told him his descendants would be as countless as the stars (Genesis 22:17). On another occasion, God told Abraham to look around him and said that that as far as his eyes could see, He (God) would give him (Genesis 13:14–15). God, our Father and creator, knew that in order for Abraham to be able to receive the blessing He had for him, He had to get him to *see* it in his mind. What are you seeing about tomorrow in your mind? If you are feeling depressed, the enemy has succeeded in convincing you that your future is bleak, and when you try to think of the future, you cannot see any positive image. But now, my friend, you can create new images with God's Word, and you will have so much life and hope spring back into your heart again. The beautiful thing is that this is not wishful thinking, but solid reality.

God's word is infallible. It is His very essence Himself. By His word were all things created, and by His word do all things consist. The extent to which you believe this is the extent to which you will experience the reality of this.

> In the beginning was the Word, and the Word was with God, and the Word was God. (John 1:1 KJV)

> For by him were all things created, that are in heaven, and that are in the earth, visible and invisible, whether they be thrones, or dominions, or principalities, or powers: all things were created by him, and for him: And he is before all things, and by him all things consist. (Colossians 1:16–17 KJV)

God's Word can be trusted, and it is to be trusted. When I was severely depressed, I could not bear to think of tomorrow. I had little or no energy for the day. I remember one day when the only scripture that kept me able to live on to the next day was a scripture in Ecclesiastes. "For to him that is joined to all the living there is hope: for a living dog is better than a dead lion" (Ecclesiastes 9:4). That made me hold on. I latched on to hope until it gave birth to faith, and then light came. There are many other scriptures that kept me, and I gazed on them in my mind and refused to lose focus. So please please, please dare to look forward! Dream impossible dreams with God's Word. See your future as beautiful as you can imagine it, regardless of how you feel. I remember singing to myself "Nke iru ka, Nke iru ka" This is my name spelt fully in my Nigerian language, Igbo. It means "The future is greater." Get a vision to motivate you to live and come through this phase. It will pass. God has good plans for you.

Spend time in prayer asking God for images and vision for your future. He will give you clear pictures that will overcome the lies of the enemy. "For I know the thoughts that I think toward you, saith the Lord, thoughts of peace, and not of evil, to give you an expected end. Then ye shall call upon me, and ye shall go and pray unto me, and I will hearken unto you. And ye shall seek me, and find me, when ye shall search for me with all your heart" (Jeremiah 29:11–13 KJV).

God has a purpose for you. Romans 8:28–30 (KJV) states, "And we know that all things work together for good to them that love God, to them who are the called according to his purpose. For whom he did foreknow, he also did predestinate to be conformed to the image of his Son, that he might be the firstborn among many brethren. Moreover whom he did predestinate, them he also called: and whom he called, them he also justified: and whom he justified, them he also glorified."

I declare now that your mind is beginning to see clearly the glorious future God has for you! I declare that your mind is filled with images of God's promises. Energy, strength, and great anticipation fills your heart right now in the name of Jesus!

Please get your eyes on God's Word daily. It could be read to you, or you could hear messages, but get your eyes on the Word too. The seeing of it, in addition to the hearing of it, is what will impart life into your mind and your entire being. Be motivated by a vision that honours God and humanity—a vision driven by love. "My son, attend to my words; incline thine ear unto my sayings. *Let them not depart from thine eyes*; keep them in the midst of thine heart. For they are life unto those that find them, and health to all their flesh" (Proverbs 4:20–22 KJV, emphasis added).

19

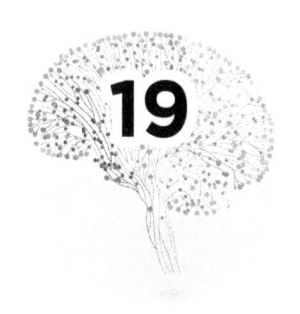

LIVING WITH JOY: LIGHT UP YOUR WORLD

I realized that when I started living not just for myself but for others, I began to have a greater sense of fulfilment, purpose, and joy. Lighting up your world speaks of reaching out to others with your unique talents, gifts, skills, experiences, and stories to help, to empower, and to bring joy to the lives of people. When you start thinking about how to solve problems for other people, how to make other people happy, and how to initiate good things for others, you will begin to experience these things for yourself. This is so key to being full of joy.

Responsibility to Shine

I remember the moment when God made it clear to me that as His children, we are truly the lights of the world; and if we do not shine, there will be darkness in the area we have been called to. Not only did He say we are light, but He went on to command us to shine as light. I have come to learn in life that when commands are given in the scriptures, they are not given to boss us around; rather, they are for our benefit. When we make it a priority to ensure we are bringing light to our world, we will see ourselves flourish.

In my past, I was rather selfish. I was always thinking about what was going on with me and how things related to me or affected me. I was really full of myself, and what this did, because I was so fixated on my problems, was to prevent me from seeing the needs around me. I was not able to use my gifts or talents to be of help to anyone, and I found myself in a vicious cycle of gloom. When you are focused on you, you will see imperfections, and your skills and gifts will lie dormant. In my medical practice, I see this pattern play out in a lot of people struggling with depression.

> Ye are the light of the world. A city that is set on an hill cannot be hid. (Matthew 5:14 KJV)

> Let your light so shine before men, that they may see your good works, and glorify your Father which is in heaven. (Matthew 5:16 KJV)

Not Complicated

Lighting up your world does not need to be complicated. It can involve anything from your everyday encounters, to volunteering in your church or community, to making a worldwide impact. The important thing is to get your focus off of you and onto others; then you will begin to experience more joy. Remember: you do not have to feel like it first. A lot of what you have to do to walk away from depression is going to have to happen without feelings first. The feelings will come.

Here are some examples of how I've learnt to light up my world that have caused results that have warmed hearts and given joy.

Being a Listening Ear

There was a day I went out shopping, and while I was in the car park, a man came to my door asking for some money. He could not speak English well, so I asked him what he needed. In my past, I would just have given him what he asked for, and that would be it. I proceeded, however, to ask about his well-being. I found out he had lost family members and was pretty much homeless. I was able to share Jesus with him and also gave him a link to where he could meet other people of his nationality and get help. He was so appreciative, and he said in his broken English with tears in his eyes, "You no understand, but you listen to me." Wow! My heart was so touched. I didn't realize how much it meant to him. I felt so blessed to have been of help. Such simple acts of kindness go such a long way and do so much for your well-being. This man left lighted up, hopeful, and I also left joyful.

Being a Helping Hand

I was out shopping again on another day and met a man in the car park. He needed to jump-start his car and wanted to use my battery. My old thinking would be "Um, sorry, I've got to shop really quickly and leave." But my new thinking said, "Hmm, this is a perfect opportunity to help and even share the love of God." So I asked him whether I could quickly shop and then we could get his car sorted, as I did not want the shop to close. He agreed. I went to shop and got back to him; we sorted out his car, and I shared Jesus with him. He was so grateful, and I was so blessed. I was filled with joy that I had been able to help that way. He said he had asked other people and was rejected.

Having my mindset focused on thinking about how I can help others with my life has radically changed me for the better. Being more compassionate at work and being more involved in my world through whatever platforms I can use to bring hope and love gives me so much joy. I encourage you to start today to wake up in the morning thinking about how you can be a blessing to someone today, no matter how little. Be consistent with this and you will experience more joy.

20

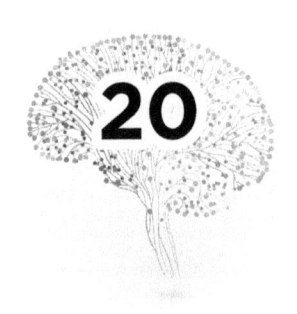

LIVING WITH JOY: ENJOYING YOUR DAYS

Life is to be enjoyed. God truly had as His intention that we enjoy our days. God made the world and then made humankind. He made it all perfect and then brought you and me into the world to be fruitful and multiply, as the scriptures record. It was all about enjoying Him and enjoying us and enjoying the life He gave us. You know, life is lived one day at a time. Life as we know it is occurring right now and right here in this moment. Yesterday has gone, and tomorrow is yet to come, but today is here! A lot of the time, people are stuck in yesterday or caught up with tomorrow. They forget today, and life just passes them by. They do not notice the goodness of God in their today. They do not see His mercy in today or recognize His blessing in today.

You only get today once, and today, just like every other day the Lord has made, is to be rejoiced in and be glad in. Every day comes with the sure mercies of God. Every day is a day to see great things happen in small or large ways. I think that if we begin to celebrate today and accord today all the excitement, the commitment for expectation, the drive, the passion, the laughter, and the expression of gratitude it avails the opportunity of showing, we will experience more joy through our days. The beautiful thing is that this will add up to a beautiful life filled with joy.

There were times in my past when, because something went wrong at the start of the day, I would be so sad throughout the day, and that day would literally go down the drain. What a waste. I am on an ever-increasing journey of joy, but I tell you I am certainly not where I used to be before. This is for you too!

Depression hits worst in the morning. It is usually the toughest time of the day. But hey, remember when you wake up that those first thoughts that come at you do not have to take control of you. They will take control of you only if you yield to them. You can decide the types of thoughts that you will yield to.

As David said in Psalm 118:24 (NIV), "This is the day the Lord has made; We will rejoice and be glad in it." Say this to yourself, and remember to say it loud.

Everything we have been given is for us to enjoy. Having the ability to enjoy our lives is a mindset. Choose to see why and how you can enjoy your day. Paraphrased, 1 Timothy 6:17 (NKJV) states, "God gives us richly all things to enjoy." So everything we have has been given to us to enjoy and not complain about. There are things we can do to enjoy our days more. Begin to think of things you would normally do for enjoyment, and make plans to do them. Even as you do the mundane things of the day—or, let me say, the things we would usually call mundane—decide to see those activities from a different perspective. Look at them from a perspective of gratitude, for instance, for the ability to do them. Relish your food, notice the breeze, be aware of the sun, take note of the awesomeness of creation, be inspired by the sounds all around you, and just glorify God.

What are your hobbies? Play a song and dance to it. Go to work with a sense of purposely enjoying what you do. Remind yourself why you got that job. Look at your spouse and think about how great and wonderful he or she is, how glad you are to have your spouse, all your spouse's gifts, and all the reasons you smile when you see and enjoy your spouse. The children are not left out here. When they make a fuss, get noisy, or run around and make a mess, take time to run around with them, scream with them, and laugh with them. Enjoy their company and savour their presence, because when they are not there, you will appreciate the joy they brought to you.

A friend of mine recently told me that she had recently just told herself she was not going to complain again about her kids. She was going to be more intentional about enjoying them. She said she started noticing things that she had been missing when she allowed herself to feel frustrated, such as the way her younger daughter's face would light up when they played and a number of other things that caused her to enjoy them more.

Enjoying Our Children

I'll just say something more about our children here, and I believe God has impressed this on my heart to share. His Word says that children are a blessing and that the fruit of the womb is His reward. He says that the man that has children is joyful (Psalm 127:3–5 NLT, paraphrased). This is not the perception the world paints to us. Let us not call a curse what God has called a blessing. Don't embrace complaining about your children or any good thing in your life. In fact, Deuteronomy 28:41 (KJV) says that the man who is under the curse will not enjoy his children. A lot of us are complaining and unthankful not just about our children but also about so many other things in life, and this allows the enemy to rob us of our joy.

Recently, when my son would wake up in the morning, I would find my thoughts saying, "Oh dear, he is up." But when I noticed this, I decided to change that response, and when he wakes up and comes to our door, I now say out loud, "Yay! My blessing is up." And this has changed how I feel about him waking up in the morning to come to my room, allowing me to enjoy him more. I truly believe that as we embrace God's perspectives and change our mindsets to His mindset, we will experience more joy in our everyday lives.

Don't wait for a wedding day or some other memorable occasion before you enjoy your days. Those events happen on Saturdays or Sundays like every other Saturday or Sunday. What makes the difference is the importance you ascribe to it and your mindset towards it. Every day can be special when you wake up knowing it is another day to experience the love of the living God, another day to know He is thinking about you, and another day to enjoy and savour His gift of life for you. Stay on the positive side of life daily. It does not matter how bleak it feels now, I tell you; the light you are seeing will shine brighter and brighter, and the darkness will dissipate.

From the deepest depths of depression, nothing can stop the laughter from coming back to your mouth. Even if it feels as if you are faking it now, I encourage you to laugh out loud. Be determined to embrace and stir up the joy of the Lord that is within your spirit. Then go have a bath or take a shower. Play music; go jogging and put yourself out there. Sooner than you know, you will begin to see the tangible results of that joy overflowing in you.

Psalm 68:3 (KJV) states, "But let the righteous be glad; let them rejoice before God: yea, let them exceedingly rejoice." The more I study joy, the more I see that committing to being joyful through the day honours God. The scriptures below show that joy was expected from the people because the day was considered to be holy. Well, what kind of day would you call holy? I would say any day the Lord has made is holy; therefore, it is my reasonable service to honour Him with remaining joy throughout the day. It's a wonderful expectation from us by God, I must say! And it is clearly for our benefit!

> This day is holy unto the Lord your God; mourn not, nor weep. (Nehemiah 8:9 KJV, paraphrased)

> Then he said unto them, Go your way, eat the fat, drink the sweet, and send portions unto them for whom nothing is prepared: for this day is holy unto our Lord: neither be ye sorry; for the joy of the Lord is your strength. (Nehemiah 8:10 KJV)

21

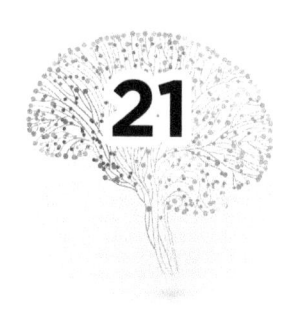

OVERCOMING DEPRESSION AND LIVING WITH JOY: A MEDICAL PERSPECTIVE

I have written this chapter to give you a combination of my thoughts and experiences from my medical perspective and the influence of God's Word. This chapter is to show you the physical side of things. All I will share is what God Himself has taught me through the years. As you read, you will see how spiritual things influence physical things, and you will be able to connect preceding chapters to the physical symptoms you may feel. You will also be able to see how you can take steps physically in response to God's Word that will bring you out of the pit of depression.

Depression: A State of Mental Stress

When a person is depressed, he or she is under extreme states of stress in the mind. Stress has a huge impact on the physical body. Stress is a state of the mind that causes physical changes in the body. When you are stressed, there is a release of chemicals that cause these changes (e.g. adrenaline and cortisol). When these hormones are produced for prolonged periods, they can cause significant harm. When you and I are relaxed, peaceful, and happy, we are usually producing hormones such as serotonin and dopamine, which help us feel a sense of overall well-being. This is why we prescribe medications like selective serotonin reuptake inhibitors (SSRIs), which help to allow for increased levels of serotonin in the system, to achieve a better mood for the patient.

It is important that you make the connection that the state of your mind has an impact on your body, to understand why it is vitally necessary to getting out of depression.

I would like you to see what modern science offers as solutions to dealing with stress and see the direct link to what the scriptures have already taught us. I share this so you can see that God has given us the blueprint for a life full of joy and peace and that we do not have to wait for science to catch up, because this life of joy and peace is found in God—the author of life and the God of all peace.

What Is Stress?

Stress is the body's response when a person feels threatened. The threat could be either real or perceived. This stress response, if allowed to persist, can cause significant physical problems. Remember that depression is characterized by persistent stress.

As a doctor, there are lots of physical ailments I see daily for which I am unable to find a physical cause, but when I look more into the patient's mental state, it is clear that there is a link to underlying stress.

Symptoms of Stress

What may be a stressor for one individual may not be a stressor for another person. However, when we are experiencing any of the following, it is a clue that we may be experiencing stress:

1. Headaches
2. Muscle Tension or pain
3. Dizziness
4. Sleep problems
5. Feeling tired all the time
6. Eating too much or too little
7. Racing thoughts
8. Constant worrying
9. Difficulty concentrating
10. Difficulty making decisions
11. Irritability
12. Being overwhelmed
13. Being anxious or fearful
14. Lacking in self-esteem

The Physical Impact of Stress

From my personal experience, my clinical practice, and my ongoing current studies in neuroscience, I have come to understand that the link between mental stress and the physical body cannot be overemphasized. It is important that we, as God's children, learn not just to manage stress but also to live free of it.

A Bit on My Personal Experience

When I went through severe depression thirteen years ago (which is a state of significant mental Stress), I experienced physical symptoms including, severe acne, a viral rash due to low immunity, poor appetite, significant weight loss, headaches, poor sleep, poor concentration and more. Coming through this successfully by the power of God's love and the application of God's word in dealing with my mental stress at the time, I realized how vitally important it is for us as believers to be more mentally aware and responsible for managing our mental states.

What Does Stress Do to the Body?

Stress causes a chemical reaction in the body that results in the production of chemicals like cortisol, adrenalin etc., in levels that are very unhealthy for the body. For example, increased levels of these hormones will cause the following effects:

Immediately ...

1. Heart pounding
2. Raised blood pressure
3. Quicker Breathing
4. Tense Muscles

Over Time ...

If the response to the stressor is not managed effectively and the person remains in a state of stress, this can cause major problems long-term, including:

1. Diabetes
2. Obesity
3. Altered immunity; causing increased risk for cancer, allergies and illness
4. Irritable bowel syndrome; colitis
5. Heart disease
6. Problems with fertility
7. Chronic fatigue syndrome (i.e. tired all the time)
8. Depression
9. Sleep problems
10. Dementia
11. Thyroid problems

And more.

This is why we there are many medical problems we do not find obvious causes for.

Practical Tips for Living Stress Free

Understanding that stress leads to and persists under the state of depression, I share with you here tips that are offered from the medical perspective to reduce stress, and I connect them with the truths I shared earlier with you in previous chapters. My prayer is that your mind gets the light it needs to clearly see what steps you need to take to forge ahead and get through successfully.

The tips I share here about reducing stress and effectively dealing with depression are available on the National Health Service (NHS) website. As I mentioned earlier, I have expressed them through the lens of the Word of God.

Meditation and Mindfulness

As believers, we need to become more mentally aware of our thoughts. I will not recommend secular practises of meditation, but I will recommend God's idea for meditation and mindfulness for the believer: "Thou wilt keep him in perfect peace, whose *mind* is stayed on thee: because he trusteth in thee" (Isaiah 26:3 KJV, emphasis added). During moments of stress, we can learn to be mentally alert to God's presence and love and His Word concerning the situation. Please let me show you what I believe meditation and mindfulness should look like for the believer in contrast to what it looks like in the secular world.

<u>What Do Meditation and Mindfulness Mean for the Believer?</u>

In the past, words involving the mind, such as "meditation" and "mindfulness", would cause me to shy away because of concerns regarding strange links to all sorts of secular practices, and rightly so. However, the states of our minds are very important to God and our transformation walks as believers. God expects us to be conscious of the state of our minds, and He expects us to meditate, but He does not expect us to do so the way the world does it, as you'll see in the scriptures below.

> Thou wilt keep him in perfect peace, whose *mind* is stayed on thee: because he trusteth in thee. (Isaiah 26:3 KJV, emphasis added)

> And do not be conformed to this world, but be transformed by the renewing of your *mind*, that you may prove what is that good and acceptable and perfect will of God. (Romans 12:2 NKJV, emphasis added)

> This book of the law shall not depart out of thy mouth; but thou shalt *meditate* therein day and night, that thou mayest observe to do according to all that is written therein: for then thou shalt make thy way prosperous, and then thou shalt have good success. (Joshua 1:8, emphasis added)

The scriptures above show that your peace is strongly linked to what your mind is focused on and that your transformation is directly linked to how much you have renewed your mind.

You would agree that we should be doing something with our minds, wouldn't you? Basically, meditation and mindfulness are not new to us in the kingdom of God, but it is a totally different practice and experience for the believer.

What Do Meditation and Mindfulness Look Like for the Believer versus the World?

I'll show you a contrast between what believers should be doing with their minds when challenged with stress as compared to what the world teaches. Here goes!

Step 1

The world says: Sit still, get quiet

God says: "BE Still and Know I am God" (Psalm 46:10).

God has told us that in the midst of whatever challenges we are facing, we are to calm down, settle down, and literally be still and *know* He is God—not *feel* He is God. That happens in the mind first, and then feelings follow. We need to learn to *know* first before seeking feelings. As 1 John 4:16 says, we have *known* and *believed* the love of God.

Let the knowledge settle your heart. Bring your thoughts to a place of calm realization that He is God! And if He is God, then He is everything His Word says He is to you. That should calm you down in a jiffy!

Step 2

The world says: focus on your breathing as you inhale and exhale.

God says—"Keep your MIND STAYED ON ME" (Isaiah 26:3). This means you are to focus on God, not on your breathing.

You need to focus on the truth and reality that He is right there in the now, dwelling in you by His Spirit, and that He loves you and His Word is real for you in that moment. He is speaking to you, and if you listen, you'll hear Him speak to your Spirit. So focus on

His present presence in you, His love for you, and His Word to you for that moment. Listen; He is always, always there! He said He will never leave you or forsake you.

Step 3

The world says: Notice when your mind has wandered, and bring it back to focusing on your breath.

God says: "*Casting down imaginations*, and every high thing that exalteth itself against the knowledge of God, and bringing into *captivity every thought to the obedience of Christ*" (2 Corinthians 10:5, emphasis added).

God also says, in Philippians 4:8, "Finally, brethren, whatsoever things are *true*, whatsoever things are *honest*, whatsoever things are *just*, whatsoever things are *pure*, whatsoever things are *lovely*, whatsoever things are *of good report*; if there be *any virtue*, and if there *be any praise*, think on these things" (emphasis added).

Clearly God wants you to have an active role in choosing your thoughts carefully and making sure they are in line with His Word, which is truth. So when your thought wanders, bring it back to His Word that brings peace to your heart.

Step 4

The world says: Well, different people suggest different things going forward, but mostly they suggest trying to keep the mind focused on present reality.

God says: Meditate on His Word day and night.

Interestingly, He tells Joshua not to let His Word depart from his mouth. The word translated as "meditate" here in the Bible refers to muttering under one's breath. Interestingly, God wants us to speak during moments when we spend time with Him in His presence, meditating. Vocalize those words of comfort He gives you in those moments. For example, "Father, I thank you that you love me", "Father, I thank you that you have not given me the spirit of fear, so I refuse to fear."

Action

Essentially, keep your mind and thoughts focused on God's presence, love, Word, and promises. Meditate on His Word and be mindful of Him.

Take Control of Your Thoughts

The website for the National Health Service (NHS), which I work in, advises "Taking Control" of one's thoughts. I would say that it is key to realize that you are not a victim of the stressor, but you can choose your response. You can take control of your thoughts. Doing so is not so much about what is happening but more about how you are responding to the situation. Ask yourself questions regarding your perception and mindset towards what is happening. For example, are you thinking the worst?

We can do this especially because we have the fruit of self-control. We have been told in scripture to take our thoughts captive, making them subject to God's Word (2 Corinthians 10:5). So what does the Word say we should think?

Philippians 4:8 is a good thought screen. Think thoughts that are true, noble, right, pure, lovely, admirable, excellent, and praiseworthy. Don't let your thoughts run wild and make you feel overwhelmed. God is not the author of confusion but is rather the author of peace (1 Corinthians 14:33).

Action

Retain a positive outlook, simplify tasks, prioritize, write tasks down, and create an achievable plan to address them. Think along the lines of best possible outcomes and imagine the best. Focus on the good. Have a Philippians 4:8 mindset.

Develop the Habit of Casting Your Cares

This is a privilege for us. The NHS advice is to "accept what you have control over and accept what you cannot change". Praise God, we can focus on our part and leave other things with God, because we know God and are known by Him (1 Corinthians 8:3). I suggest that when you find yourself getting stressed over something, you should stop yourself, identify the issue, read the scriptures that relate to that issue, mentally leave that with God, and move on with other things, trusting that He will sort it out. Cast it upon Him, and don't pick it up again by worrying. "Therefore humble yourselves under the mighty hand of God, that he may exalt you in due time, CASTING ALL YOUR CARE upon Him, for he careth for you" (1 Peter 5:6–7 KJV). Habits can take up to eight weeks to be established. You are building new neural pathways. So be persistent in developing this new habit of casting cares and not worrying or carrying them by yourself.

Action

Relax, don't worry, and learn to trust God.

Connect with People and Help People

The NHS advises increasing connections with people and seeking to help other people. Science has shown that when you do this, your neural networks form better. Taking the focus off you and seeking to be a blessing to someone else gives you perspective, relieves you, and frees you from the stressor. As a believer, the summary of what I see being projected here is science catching up with the commandment to *love*. It is evident that "walking in love" towards people will keep you mentally alert and whole; 1 Corinthians 1: 4–13 expands on how to walk in love. Chapter 12 of this book, which is about living with joy and abiding in love, explains the spiritual foundation for this reality.

Action

Call family or friends, volunteer, and do someone a favour daily. Do not stay isolated. Forgive, and keep no record of wrongs.

Do Things You Enjoy

The NHS advises taking out time to do things we enjoy. Remember: scripture says that He gives us all things to richly enjoy (1 Timothy 6:17). As such, we should be actively seeking to enjoy our lives. Take out time to enjoy every day. Enjoy family, work, and life as a whole. Take out time to enjoy creation. I explained in detail the spiritual foundation for this in chapter 18, which is about enjoying your days.

Action

Be intentional about your favourite fun activities. Live in the moment, enjoy every bit of your day, and take in the beautiful sights of creation.

Be Goal Oriented

The NHS advises setting goals and challenges for yourself. Give yourself targets to learn something new. For example, learn a new language or a new sport in order to avoid living passively and also to help build confidence and resilience. I would add that at the core of this is living with a sense of purpose. Living with a dream or vision for yourself in mind will motivate you daily. To be more goal oriented, I will encourage you to create vision boards, which are images of things you would like to accomplish that are placed around you (for example, on your walls). This will stir you and cause you to be motivated, resulting in higher energy levels whenever you see them. Be motivated by a vision that honours God and humanity, and that is driven by love.

> And The Lord answered me, and said, write the vision, and make it plain upon tables, that he may run that readeth it. (Habakkuk 2:2 KJV)
>
> Where there is no vision, the people perish. (Proverbs 29:18a KJV)

In chapter 17 of this book, which is about the power of vision, the spiritual foundation for this reality is clearly explained.

Action

Create a vision board. Set goals that excite you. Include pictures and words indicating what you want to achieve.

Be Thankful

Research shows that people who are more grateful report more life satisfaction and less stress. Have a grateful mindset. This will help you have a healthy and wholesome perspective on life. In chapter 14, which deals with the power of praise and thanksgiving, the spiritual foundation for this is explained.

Action

Take out time to thank God for His goodness and to thank and appreciate people.

Live Loved

In secular terms, the mindset of loving oneself is called self-love. However, I like to call it Live Loved. It is a mindset of knowing you are loved. This gives you security in your identity as a loved child of God and confidence in who He says you are. This frees you from the stress and tension of any sense of negative self-perception causing low self-esteem, which in extreme cases can lead to issues like self-harm. This enables you to develop the gifts in you and to seek to be all you were created to be, without fear. Both chapter 3 and chapter 13, which are on freedom from a poor self-image and knowing your identity, respectively, give the spiritual foundation for the truth about what the world calls self-love versus Living Loved.

Action

Write a description of who you are based on the scriptures, and affirm this by verbalizing it daily.

Sleep, Exercise, Eating Well

Dealing with stress will ultimately help you sleep better and enable you to be more motivated to exercise and eat well. Also, sleeping better, exercising, and eating well will

help you reduce stress. Most of the patients I see who are struggling with sleep are struggling because they are not getting any sleep or are sleeping and waking up unrefreshed because they are stressed, anxious, and ultimately depressed. Depressed people are often unable to sleep, are not motivated to exercise, and lack healthy appetites. Putting into practice all that has been shared so far in this book will greatly help.

I remember not being able to sleep during my time spent suffering from depression, and I would tell myself that God gives His beloved good sleep (Psalm 127:2); thus I avoided worrying about not being able to sleep, knowing it would come. It is so key not to worry about being unable to sleep, as this only makes things worse.

Medications for Depression

I will say here that medications can be helpful, but the more you are able to do without medications, the better for you. Medications also do not deal with toxic thought patterns. As such, the reason why a wound occurred will continue to cause more wounds if it is not addressed. Whether you are on medications or not, focus on dealing with the thoughts, and then the medication will help even better.

22

LIVING WITH JOY: KNOWING YOU ARE NOT ALONE

I have saved the best for last. Right now it may feel as though you are so far gone, and navigating your way out of this condition may seem insurmountable and impossible, but I have good news for you. You are not alone. The responsibility to get out of where you are right now does not rest entirely on you. You have the Holy Spirit. He is your helper, your teacher, your counsellor, your psychologist, your psychiatrist, your doctor, your guide, and your Shepherd. The Holy Spirit is God Himself in you. He proceeds from the Father (John 15:26).

Jesus said the following about the Holy Spirit, who was going to come when He left.

> And I will pray the Father, and he shall give unto you another Comforter, that he may abide with you forever; even the Spirit of truth; whom the world cannot receive, because it seeth him not, neither knoweth him: ye know him; for he dwelleth with you, and shall be in you. (John 14:16–17 KJV)

But the comforter which is the Holy Ghost, whom the Father will send in my name, he shall teach you all things, and bring all things to your remembrance, whatsoever I have said unto you. (John 14:26)

Howbeit when he, the Spirit of truth, is come, he will guide you into all truth: for he shall not speak of himself; but whatsoever he shall hear, that shall he speak; and he will shew you things to come. (John 16:13)

As long as you keep following His leading, He will get you out.

Knowing the Voice of the Spirit

Learning His voice is so key. The more you get acquainted with the written Word, the more you will know when He is speaking to you. There will be times when a thought will come to you and you will know it is not you but Him speaking to you. Listen for Him. He is in you, and He is always with you. He never leaves, and He speaks to you. His voice always speaks peace to your heart. His voice is always in line with the written Word of God. He got me out of my mess and brought me to safety, and I know He wants to do this with you.

Praying in Other Tongues

When you were born again by believing in your heart and confessing with your mouth the death and resurrection of Jesus for your forgiveness and justification, the Holy Spirit came to dwell in you. There is more that He can do in you and with you when you get baptized with the Holy Spirit. I am not a theologian; I speak only from experience and what I see written in the Word. When I was severely depressed, my mind played tricks on me. I had delusions and hallucinations at one point. My mind was not in a good place at all, so praying became very difficult. I remember my sister reminding me one day to pray more in other tongues. This was so key for me in getting out of it all, because when you pray in other tongues, you are praying directly from your spirit to God. You are expressing your emotions and desires perfectly to God while bypassing your mind, and the Holy Spirit Himself prays for us by giving us these words.

I know it's tough for some to understand, but if you just let go of your reasoning and receive this, wow, you will experience God as you never have before. I still remember watching TBN when I was younger. I got excited about the message being preached on one occasion on TV. The minister then prayed for people who wanted to receive the baptism of the Holy Spirit, and I opened up to this. I said the prayer, and I started speaking by faith. It seemed strange at first, but then I went on and on, and since then, I have never stopped.

I remember one of the hardest nights I had during my trial of depression. For the first time in my life, I prayed all night in tongues, nonstop. I did this because I felt as though I was holding on for dear life. I cannot fully explain what happened, but at that moment I experienced, for the first time in my life, the gifts of the Spirit in me. I started knowing things about people that I could not have known on my own. This is called the word of knowledge. The information was for their benefit. The point I am making here is that praying in other tongues is a vital ability the Lord has given us, and I pray you receive and make good use of this gift.

> Likewise the Spirit also helpeth our infirmities: for we know not what we should pray for as we ought: but the Spirit itself maketh intercession for us with groanings which cannot be uttered. (Romans 8:26)

> For he that speaketh in an unknown tongue speaketh not unto men, but unto God: for no

man understandeth him; howbeit in the spirit he speaketh mysteries. (1 Corinthians 14:2)

The Holy Spirit is here to help you.

Prayer

I want to pray with you right now that you will receive the baptism of the Holy Spirit and will be able to speak in other tongues and pray your way out of depression and into constant victory and joy.

Dear Holy Spirit, I ask that you rest on the person reading these words now, and I ask that as they begin to speak, you give them utterance.

Begin to speak now in other tongues by faith. Speak sounds and words from your heart as they come; you can just let yourself go, express yourself freely, and know that you are speaking directly to God. Praise God! you are on your way to victory!

Even if you haven't taken this step now, God loves you, and He knows how to get you free. Stay in the Word and talk to Him in the best way you know how. The Holy Spirit will never

leave you or forsake you.

ABOUT THE AUTHOR

Dr Nkiru Oluwatosin is a primary care physician in England, where she attends to patients of all ages and spectrums of illness. She is certified by Harvard University in the fundamentals of neuroscience. She is a mental health first aider trained by Mental Health First Aid England. She is currently running a leadership-focused fellowship in mental health under Health Education England.

She is the founder of Heirmindset, a UK-based charity with Reg n0. 1194193 (www.heirmindset.org). The charity runs a Christian faith-based mind clinic which she hosts. It is an interactive virtual platform with which she helps people win in their minds with God's Word. The platform has a virtual community presence on the Telegram app, which is open to people wanting to be trained to have a mindset to live with an unshakable identity in Christ, peace, and joy.

Dr Nkiru is a teacher of God's Word. She is a member of the teaching team at her local church. She is happily married to her husband, Dr Mayowa Oluwatosin, and they have been blessed with a lovely son, Fijinoluwa. Dr Nkiru enjoys family, fun, dance, laughter, art, all things bright and beautiful, and, most of all, seeing God's will done on the earth.

Connect and share testimonies with Dr Nkiru and her team by following her on Instagram (@dr_nkiru), subscribing to the YouTube channel "Mind Clinic with Dr Nkiru" and by connecting on the Telegram app by searching *"Mind Clinic with Dr Nkiru"*.

Lightning Source UK Ltd.
Milton Keynes UK
UKHW010237091221
395309UK00001B/125